REINVENTING DEVELOPMENT

Reinventing Development

Aid Reform and Technologies of Governance in Ghana

LORD MAWUKO-YEVUGAH

Ghana Institute of Management and Public Administration, Accra, Ghana

Routledge
Taylor & Francis Group
LONDON AND NEW YORK

First published 2014 by Ashgate Publishing

Published 2016 by Routledge
2 Park Square, Milton Park, Abingdon, Oxfordshire OX14 4RN
52 Vanderbilt Avenue, New York, NY 10017

First issued in paperback 2016

Routledge is an imprint of the Taylor & Francis Group, an informa business

British Library Cataloguing in Publication Data
A catalogue record for this book is available from the British Library

The Library of Congress has cataloged the printed edition as follows:
Mawuko-Yevugah, Lord.
Reinventing development : aid reform and technologies of governance in Ghana / by Lord Mawuko-Yevugah.
pages cm. – (Contemporary african politics)
Includes bibliographical references and index.
ISBN 978-1-4724-2674-1 (hardback)
1. Economic development–Political aspects–Ghana. 2. Ghana–Politics and government–2001- 3. Ghana–Economic conditions–21st century.
I. Title.
HC1060.Z9E446 2014
338.9109667–dc23

2013048255

ISBN 13: 978-1-138-25289-9 (pbk)
ISBN 13: 978-1-4724-2674-1 (hbk)

For Yvonne, Jude and Jaden

Contents

Preface

Like other Sub-Saharan African countries, Ghana's postcolonial political history has been marked by periods of turbulence as well as relative stability. Having led the continent towards political liberation in 1957 under its charismatic, visionary and Pan-African leader, Kwame Nkrumah, Ghana also became a symbol of Africa's spectacular post-independence failure. In 1966, the Nkrumah government was overthrown in a military coup d'état. This was followed by several other coups, political uncertainty and economic collapse. In January 2001, however, Ghana made history when military strongman-turned democratically-elected President Jerry Rawlings of the National Democratic Congress (NDC) handed over power to then President-elect John Agyekum Kufuor of the opposition New Patriotic Party (NPP). This was the first peaceful change of government through the ballot box in the postcolonial political period.

A few days after taking office in January 2001, the new president, John Kufuor, through his finance minister, Yaw Osafo-Maafo, told parliament that the country was in dire economic straits resulting from mismanagement and bad policies of the previous government.[1] Accordingly, the new government, he added, would access the Heavily Indebted Poor Countries (HIPC) initiative by the World Bank and the International Monetary Fund (IMF).[2] The HIPC initiative had been introduced by the World Bank and the IMF in 1994 as an instrument for granting debt relief to qualified developing countries. Opting for the HIPC initiative effectively signaled national bankruptcy and the inability of the country to service its bilateral and multilateral debts. Many Ghanaians were outraged by this revelation and wanted answers not only from the officials of the past administration but also from the donor agencies that had for almost twenty years showered praises upon the Rawlings-led regime for its ostensibly prudent management of the economy.[3] What was notable to many was the fact that officials at the World Bank's local office in Accra swiftly denounced the past government's economic policies and commended the decision by the new Kufuor government to access the HIPC initiative.[4]

My initial segue into this discussion began around the time I started working as a journalist with an Accra-based *Business and Financial Times* newspaper in 2001. Given the widespread public outcry following the revelations on the state of the economy, I decided to follow-up on the many questions and concerns being directed

---

1 Government of Ghana (Budget and Financial Statement), 2001.

2 Government of Ghana (Budget and Financial Statement), 2001.

3 Ghana News Agency (GNA), 2001.

4 World Bank, 2002.

at the World Bank and other donor agencies. When I met the World Bank Country Director, I asked him to explain the about-face and why his organization could now turn to criticize the past government for poor management of the economy when it had for years given the same government high marks. Why did anybody not raise the red flag when the government was backtracking on the economic recovery measures? Was this not part of the rationale for having a country office working with local clients to ensure aid money was put into good use? Or is it a mere public relations exercise aimed at courting the new government? At the time, the World Bank Country Director's response was telling: 'Well, you know, the World Bank does not tell countries what to do; we don't interfere in the internal affairs of countries; the government chose to over-spend during an election year and took many economically unwise but politically prudent decisions, which we couldn't possibly overrule.'[5]

Like many Ghanaians, I was troubled by the contradictory rhetoric of our 'development partners.' I was also troubled by the inconsistencies of the government. The general hope was that with a brand new government with a new slogan, 'development in freedom',[6] at least the long suffering Ghanaians could now hope for better days. How premature these hopes were. Perhaps, the speed with which the Kufuor government had gone to the Washington institutions and the party's own self-confessed centre-right ideological inclinations should have alerted all in Ghana that despite the change of guard in the corridors of power, the Western-aid dependent and donor-controlled policy terrain that had come to define the country's political economy remained very much intact. What we also failed to grasp at the time was the fact that successive postcolonial governments since Nkrumah had become implicated in the neocolonial interventionist ideas and policies that were integral elements of the early modernization and the neoliberal development agenda.[7]

Born in a small village in south eastern Ghana in the 1970s, I belong to a generation of Ghanaians who missed both the era of colonialism and the victory of the anti-colonial movement. My generation, nonetheless, has come to represent the beneficiaries, victims, challenges and opportunities of independent nationhood and the neocolonial interventionist policies of an ostensibly postcolonial era. By the time I left my hometown to enroll in a secondary school in the mid-1980s, Ghana, like most African countries, had had its fair share of what was increasingly called the postcolonial 'crisis.' In terms of its economy, the country was already in the surgical theater of the World Bank and the IMF for diagnosis of its economic ailment, and had been prescribed a treatment that included a good dosage of neoliberal economic reform policies. And by the time I completed secondary school

5 Business and Financial Times, 2002; Business in Africa Magazine, 2001.

6 New Patriotic Party (NPP), 2000. Note the similarity between this slogan and Amartya Sen's ground-breaking work, *Development as Freedom* (Oxford: Oxford University Press, 1999).

7 See Mawuko-Yevugah, 2013.

in 1992, the country had gone from 'a hopeless' case to a 'success story' in the estimation of the Bank and the IMF.[8] The military regime of Jerry Rawlings which had been in power for over a decade was also in the process of metamorphosing into a political party in order to contest the general elections of that year under a new multi-party constitution.

In the meantime, so called 'successes' of the economic recovery program did not seem to be translating into important areas of social development and well being like education, healthcare and agriculture. For instance, the introduction of cost recovery measures, especially in tertiary institutions, on at least one occasion, resulted in a year-long closure of all public universities due to students' unrest. This incident, which occurred during the 1994/95 academic year, derailed the academic calendar and created a huge backlog of qualified students who had to spend years on the 'waiting list' for admission into the universities. In the health sector, a 'cash and carry' policy was introduced as a cost-recovery mechanism. The downside of this policy, no matter the case for its introduction, was the inhumane treatment meted out to patients, including expectant mothers, accident victims and the aged who were denied treatment on the grounds of inability to pay. In the agriculture sector, the removal of subsidies on basic agricultural tools, equipment and facilities on one hand and the provision of incentives for cash crop farmers on the other, undermined food crop production, resulting in perennial food shortages.

In September 1996, I finally entered the University of Ghana after two years on the waiting list. By this time the student movement and the popular protests against the Rawlings-led administration had become widespread. Like many other cohorts and contemporaries, I became an active member in both the University of Ghana's student government and the wider National Union of Ghana Students (NUGS). It was apparent that the economic recovery programs facilitated by the international financial institutions had failed to address the myriad of problems faced by a country that had only recently emerged from years of colonial occupation. The increasing cost of education and the growing army of unemployed university graduates became the rallying grounds for my generation's opposition to policies seen to be inimical to our future and that of our country.

That day in March 2000 was one any child who had lived through the 'revolutionary' years of the Rawlings-led military administrations of the 1970s and 1980s could only dream about. That was the day I stepped onto the podium at the athletics field at the University of Ghana to receive my first class honors degree from President Jerry Rawlings. When Rawlings first burst onto Ghana's political scene in 1979, I was a young boy, who had only started formal education a year earlier. Ever since, Rawlings has remained a sort of mythic figure in Ghana's postcolonial political history and a hero to many people, especially those who were old enough to live through the military dictatorships of the 1970s. I used to listen to my mother and other elderly folks praising Rawlings for liberating the country from the misrule of successive leaders after Kwame Nkrumah, the

8 Tsikata, 2001.

founding President. So as I stood on that podium holding his hands, many things went through my mind. Looking back I wished I had the courage to ask him at least one question regarding some of his policies and to find out if he really believed that those policies were in the best interest of the country. For here was a man who, on one hand, proclaimed his belief in social justice, probity, and accountability[9] and held himself out as defender of the less privileged, yet[10] at the same time became a darling of Western countries and institutions because he implemented their harsh policy prescriptions.

The joy of graduation, like the euphoria that had greeted the country's attainment of political independence a few decades earlier, was short-lived. It became apparent that being a top student was not a guarantee for securing a job. Neither was it enough to proceed to graduate school given the astronomical costs. So I had to just wait and hope that an opportunity would occur. And to be sure, one did arise when I was among a handful of 'fortunate' graduates recruited by a new media outlet dedicated to business and financial journalism. It was during my time at this publication as parliamentary correspondent and later as the features and political editor that I first came into direct contact with the country's political, economic and social elites. By the time I resigned from the paper to take up an appointment as a program officer with a leading local policy think-tank, The Institute of Economic Affairs (IEA), I had experienced my fair share of disappointments. I saw first-hand the waste and, above all, the hypocrisy of the new political elites who had campaigned on the platform of 'positive change'[11] to win the December 2000 general elections.

It was also during the period at the *Business and Financial Times* that I became interested in the intricacies of international development cooperation. I was invited to a number of policy dialogues with donor agencies, policy-makers and civil society groups. By this time, Ghana had again emerged as a front-runner in the implementation of a new aid framework, which was introduced towards the end of the 1990s. As mentioned earlier, the new Kufuor government did not waste time in signing up for the HIPC initiative. With this came the windfall of multilateral and bilateral debt relief. Once again, Ghana has emerged as a 'star pupil'—this time with a recent success at democratic good governance to boot. At the IEA, I became the point-person for facilitating a series of policy forums involving 'development partners' and other 'stakeholders.' This, in addition to my role as a research assistant, offered me the opportunity to interact with all the key players from the

9 'Probity,' 'accountability' and 'integrity' became part of Ghana's political lexicon during the Rawlings era. See also Shillington, 1992.

10 Between June and September 1979 when Rawlings presided over the Armed Forces Revolutionary Council (AFRC) military junta, eight senior military officers, including three former heads of state were infamously executed by firing squad for their alleged mismanagement of the economy and corruption. For detailed analyses see Oquaye, 1980; Shillington, 1992; Dzorgbo, 2001.

11 NPP, 2000.

donor community, the political elites and policy-makers and the bourgeoning civil society community. At the time, I did not stop to wonder if the latest aid initiatives being promoted by the same Western donors offered any drastic departures from the earlier ones that Ghana and other African countries were forced to adopt. Sometimes, I wondered whether what was unfolding with the incorporation, if not cooptation, of civil society groups into the new aid mechanisms was nothing more than a new elites' consensus. The more I observed and interacted with the various stakeholders in Ghana's development policy-making process and tried to make sense of the contradictions associated with some of the claims made in support of the new policy interventions, the more I knew I needed to put my personal and professional experiences into a bigger context, in the form of a concentrated research agenda.

In a nutshell, this book concerns questions that have preoccupied me for over a decade and although it has taken me a few years to complete, it is a culmination of a life-long experience of personal struggles, investigative journalism, policy analysis, field research, observations and activism. It has been a journey, first embarked upon by a child growing up in a remote African village with no access to good drinking water or electricity, who went to school barefooted, and sat under a mango tree for classes. Yet, despite the prevalence of afro-pessimism, that same child was able to live a childhood dream of sitting in one of those airplanes which used to fly over the village and to be educated in some of the world's finest institutions.[12] This book is thus a chronicle of years of thinking through Ghana's postcolonial story and a serious engagement with some of the recurrent themes in this story. In this work, I grapple with serious questions regarding the idea of economic policy in relation to independent nationhood, national sovereignty and agency and the participation of the citizenry and civil society.

Along this academic journey, I have encountered many individuals who have inspired, mentored, encouraged, challenged and supported me in diverse ways. In particular, I wish to acknowledge the role of my family and many great individuals, teachers, students, colleagues and friends whom I have encountered throughout my academic journey and intellectual development in Ghana, United Kingdom, Canada, United States, South Africa and the Netherlands. I have also benefitted from the generosity and support of many individuals and institutions in the course of my academic career and during the research for this book. In particular, I am most grateful to Lisa Aubrey, Steven Ahiawordor, Joseph A. Ayee, Amos Anyimadu, Emmanuel Gyimah-Boadi, Kwesi Yankah, Shailaja Fennell, Dylan Sutherland, Malinda Smith, Andy Knight, Tom Keating, Fred Judson, Ali Abdi, Rob Aitkin, Lois Harder, Wisdom J. Tettey, Rita Abrahamsen, Janine Brodie, Meenal Shrivastava, Ruby Amable, Korblah Puplampu, Jean Mensa, Doe Adjaho, Hudzengor Amenakpor, Andreas Yevugah, Mary-Makafui Yevugah,

12 In October 2003, I left Ghana to study for a master's degree in development studies as a Commonwealth Scholar at Downing College, University of Cambridge. I proceeded to the University of Alberta in September 2004 for a doctorate in political science.

Peace Yevugah, Grace Yevugah, Esinam Yevugah, Rita Yevugah, Angelina and Angela Yevugah, James Yevugah, Shadrack Atsu Yevugah, Vicentia Kafui Dagadu, Seth Louis De-Souza, Kenneth De-souza, Bernard Okpattah, Dzixorse Okpattah, Bernice Mawusi Okpattah, J.T.K. Quaye, Adelaide Quaye, Harriet Quaye, Bridget Quaye, Denis K. Agbenyadzi, Victor Ashiagbor, Michael Okyerefo, Felix Deyegbe, Mathew Kudo, Paul Kpogli, Richmond Sekyi, Clemence Agbonyitor, Bawa Faisal, George Kwaku Yeboah, Michael Tugli, Tassah Tapha, Fidel Lamptey, Hill Abigail Barker, Sylvia Klu, Yaw Saffu, Kwesi Jonah, Michael Kpessa, Richard Adjei, Geta Striggner-Quartey, Franklin Cudjoe, Providence Mireku, Emmanuel Akwetey, Richard Aidoo, William Dorgbadzi, Jake Addison, Ben Dotse Malor, Tekyiwaa Manuh, Akosua A. Ampofo, Jasper Ayelazuno, David Matsinhe, Edwin Etieyibo, Vi Valerie, Paul Ugor, Megan Mackenzie, Jay Johnson, Shawn Hashmi, Amanda Chisholm, Christine Smith, Paul Nyibek, Chizoba Imoka, Isaac Odoom, Nathan Andrews, Afyare Elmi, Boniface Mgonja, Wisdom Agorde, Keli Tamakloe, Fred Ackah, Justina Dugbazah, Rod Alence, Gilbert Khadiagala, Achille Mbembe, Amy Niang, Mopeli Moshoshoe, Nomfundo Xenia Ngwenya, Nobuhle Kwanda, Ekemini Eyita, Alecia Ndlovu, Nyiko Khoza, Cayley Bowland, Mothepa Shadung, Kingsley Orievulu, Charles Ukeje, Nontokozo Setiba, Nomonde Ndwalaza, Bonga Carl Msiza, Nomzamo Zinhle Mkhabela, David Moore, Julia Steets, Jacqueline Rutte, Stefano Bellucci, Marcel Van Der Linden, Philip Osei, Samuel Bonsu, Bertha Osei-Hwedie, Joseph Darmoe, Kwabena Amoah, Afrakuma Boakye-Ansah, Naomi Marbel, Morgan Nyendu and Thina Nzo. I am very grateful to the University of Alberta International, the University of Alberta Faculty of Graduate Studies and Research as well as the Consular Corps of Edmonton for funding the project. I thank the Institute of Economic Affairs, Ghana for hosting me during the period of my field research in Ghana. I am equally grateful to the International Institute of Social History in Amsterdam, The Netherlands for providing me the perfect environment to conclude this project during my six-month tenure as SNS Research Fellow. Finally, a heartfelt gratitude and appreciation go to my loving wife Yvonne, and my children, Jude and Jaden who have been a huge source of extra energy and inspiration throughout this project. However, I alone am responsible for the contents and any shortcomings of this book.

Lord C. Mawuko-Yevugah
Amsterdam, The Netherlands
April 2014

Series Editor's Preface

Once seen only as a continent of poverty, violence and corruption, the Africa of today is a vibrant place where social forces demand representative governance; in the process generating fresh forms of complexities in the political, social and economic life of ordinary Africans. Whether what we are witnessing is a third liberation of the continent: the first from colonialism, the second from autocratic indigenous rule and now something far more different, is a work in progress.

This series seeks original approaches to furthering our understanding of the ensuing changes on the continent. The series includes work that progresses comparative analysis of African politics. It look at the full range and variety of African politics in the twenty-first century covering the changing nature of African society, gender issues, economic prosperity and poverty to the development of relations between African states, external organisations and between leaders and the people they would govern. The series aims to publish work by senior scholars as well as the best new researchers and features original research monographs, thematically strong edited collections and specialised texts.

Nana K. Poku,
Health Economics and AIDS Research Division (HEARD),
South Africa

List of Abbreviations

AFRC	Armed Forces Revolutionary Council
AU	African Union
BWIs	Bretton Woods Institutions
CBOs	Community Based Organizations
CPP	Convention Peoples Party
CSOs	Civil Society Organizations
ECA	United Nations Economic Commission for Africa
ECOWAS	Economic Community of West African States
ERP	Economic Reform Program
GBA	Ghana Bar Association
GPRS	Ghana Poverty Reduction Strategy
IFIs	International Financial Institutions
IMF	International Monetary Fund
IOs	International Organizations
LPA	Lagos Plan of Action
MCA	Millennium Challenge Account
MDAs	Ministries, Agencies and Departments
MDGs	Millennium Development Goals
MNCs	Multinational National Corporations
NDC	National Democratic Congress
NDPC	National Development Planning Commission
NEC	National Economic Committee
NEPAD	New Economic Partnership for African Development
NIEO	New International Economic Order
NLC	National Liberation Council
NPP	New Patriotic Party
NRC	National Redemption Council
NUGS	National Union of Ghana Students
OAU	Organization of Africa Unity
PNC	Peoples National Convention
PNDC	Provisional National Defence Council
PP	Progress Party
PRSPs	Poverty Reduction Strategy Papers
SAPs	Structural Adjustment Policies
SMC	Supreme Military Council
SOEs	State Owned Enterprises

TUC	Trades Union Congress
UN	United Nations
US	United States

Chapter 1
Introduction: Discourses on Aid and Development Policy Reform

For over three decades, the predominantly Western international donor community led by the two Bretton Woods Institutions (BWIs),—the World Bank and the International Monetary Fund (IMF)—has influenced and shaped the economic and development processes of countries in Sub-Saharan Africa and other regions of the global South. This dominance has been largely defined through Structural Adjustment Policies (SAPs) promoted from the late 1970s and early 1980s.[1] These policies came to be known as the 'Washington consensus,'[2] a term first used in 1989 by a World Bank economist, John Williamson, to describe a set of policies first introduced in Latin America then later, in other regions of the global South to stabilize their economies and spur on growth.[3] The structural adjustment policies also represented a form of policy conditionality whereby loans from the World Bank, IMF and regional development banks, aid from bilateral donors and even private finance became effectively conditional on the agreement by the recipient government to implement often far-reaching economic policy reforms. Broadly, the key policy instruments in the implementation of the SAPs were privatization of state enterprises and downsizing of the public sector, trade and financial liberalization, fiscal austerity and tight monetary policy to reduce inflation.[4] These measures, were aimed at stabilizing the domestic economy, make it attractive for private-sector led development and attractive to foreign direct investment. As a result, across board, the SAPs emphasized export-led growth, privatization and liberalization, and the efficiency of the free market.[5]

Many years of promoting and implementing economic restructuring in the form of structural adjustment policies however failed to transform the economies

1 For detailed discussion on the theory as well as the impact of structural adjustment policies implemented across the South since the late 1970s and early 1980s see Giles Mohan et al., 2000.

2 In his work, 'What Washington Means by Policy Reform.'(1990), John Williamson, summarized the Washington Consensus as follows: fiscal discipline, trade liberalization, macroeconomic stability, and getting prices right. These prescriptions which became fashionable in Latin America as a remedy for the region's poor economic performance became the standards for donor aid and development policy in the developing world.

3 Williamson, 1990.

4 Mohan et al., 2000.

5 Hoogvelt, 2001.

as well as the social conditions in Africa and other regions of the global South. As a result, from the middle of the 1980s, these policies became the target of sustained criticisms from within the BWIs and from outside. From within the Bretton Woods establishment, there developed an opposition to the Washington Consensus in the form of critical commentary and resignations of prominent officials.[6] The opposition of SAPs also manifested in a growing international movement for justice and debt relief, led by the anti-globalization movement and the Jubilee 2000 campaign.[7] A key criticism against the Washington Consensus policies represented by the SAPs was their failure to eradicate poverty in Africa and elsewhere in the developing world. In the contrary, these countries continued to accumulate more debt and were increasingly unable to provide basic social services.

In response to these criticisms, the international donor community, led by the World Bank and the IMF through the 1990s until today, introduced a new set of policies including the Heavily Indebted Poor Countries (HIPC) initiative, Comprehensive Development Framework (CDF), the Millennium Development Goals (MDGs) and the New Partnership for African Development (NEPAD).[8] In 1999, these new aid initiatives crystallized into the poverty reduction paper framework which is claimed to be 'comprehensive' and as having a 'long-term perspective' towards development.[9] This 'new' architecture of aid seeks to refocus international development on poverty reduction[10] and promises a new process for development lending, which would alter aid relationships by putting recipient

6 Joseph Stiglitz, the World Bank's chief economist at the time became one of the fiercest critics of the BWIs from within, calling for a 'Post-Washington Consensus.' His subsequent resignation was interpreted by many as an attempt by the Washington establishment led by the US Treasury Department and the IMF to silence internal dissent. See also Fine, 2006; Chang, 2001.

7 Peet, 2007.

8 Smith et al., 2007; Pender, 2001.

9 IMF and World Bank, 1999.

10 While 'poverty reduction' has been on the agenda of international development institutions such as the World Bank and the IMF, for a long time dating back to the 1940s, the two institutions in the past conceptualized 'poverty' within the narrow confines of GDP and economic growth (see Malinda Smith 2008) 'Rethinking Poverty in a Global Era,' in Janine Brodie and Sandra Rein (eds) *Critical Concepts: an introduction to politics (4th edition)*, Toronto: Pearson Education. There have also been attempts to mainstream poverty reduction in the international development agenda, including the 1995 Copenhagen World Summit for Social Development. The final declaration of the Copenhagen Summit and adoption of a 'Program of Action' by the donor community, including a pledge by developed countries to commit 0.7 percent of GDP to international aid was hailed as representing a new consensus on the need to put people at the center of development. This commitments have however remained mere slogans until the issues of poverty reduction and social development re-emerged on the international development agenda towards the end of the 1990s in the form of the poverty reduction strategy process and the UN's Millennium Development Goals (see Greig et al., 2007).

countries in the driver's seat of development policy making.[11] In other words, the essence of the new poverty reduction framework is to give countries in the global South the chance to develop their own development policies and to move away from what has been described as 'the one-size-fits-all' approach of SAPs.[12] Also, as a key component of the new aid agenda, or what has been referred to as 'post-Washington Consensus',[13] the poverty reduction strategy policies (PRSPs) are supposed to facilitate the engagement of civil society in the developmental process. This new framework and its emphasis on social development, at least in theory, imply a significant shift from the earlier emphasis on strict market fundamentalism and economic growth under the structural adjustment policies and the Washington Consensus. It is in that vein that some have concluded that the PRSP framework marks a departure from the past development policies promoted by BWIs to an inclusive neoliberalism.[14] The shift from the 'Washington consensus' in the form of the Structural Adjustment Policies (SAPs) to a 'post-Washington consensus' represented by the poverty reduction strategies raises a couple of interrelated questions that this book sets out to explore. The key question explored in the book is this: Has the new aid agenda enabled governmental and societal actors in countries like Ghana to assume control over their development policy agenda? Or, do the new policies represent the World Bank and the International Monetary Fund's attempt to shift from direct conditionality to a more indirect conditionality? The two international financial institutions claim that the new poverty reduction and development agenda represents a shift from top-down, to one that puts developing countries in the driver's seat of their own development policy making process.[15] Therefore, the secondary question explored in the book is this: What, if anything, is 'new' about what is now called the 'new architecture of aid'? Is it, as its critics charge, simply a replication of the neoliberal agenda of previous Western donor policies? In a nutshell, this book probes the degree to which the PRSP approach has transformed donor-recipient country relations and determines whether this 'new architecture of aid' does allow developing countries like Ghana the space to develop home-grown policies. Drawing on Ghana, the book interrogates these competing claims and examines the continuities and discontinuities in the shift

11 World Bank and IMF, 1999.

12 Zack-Williams and Mohan, 2005; Harrison, 2001.

13 The term, 'Post-Washington Consensus' was first used by Stiglitz in 1998 in relation to the emerging policy reforms spearheaded by new World Bank President, James Wolfensohn in the form of the Comprehensive Development Framework, with an emphasis on social development and broad local participation in the development policy making process. For details on 'Post-Washington Consensus' see Stiglitz, 1998; 1999; 2002.

14 Scholars such as Craig and Porter (2006) and Ruckert (2008) have interpreted the introduction of the poverty reduction framework as an attempt by the international donor community to 'bring back the social' into international development by integrating ideas of social development while maintaining the emphasis on the market and economic growth as the fundamental basis for human progress and well-being.

15 IMF and World Bank, 1999.

from the SAPs to PRSPs. It does so by probing whether or not the emphasis on 'country ownership' and 'civil society participation' translates into actual policy changes, which indeed place aid recipient countries like Ghana in the driver's seat of the development agenda. It also questions whether or not this new aid architecture with its promise of 'poverty reduction' challenges or aims to eradicate the structural inequalities within the global economy which have in many ways contributed to the high incidence of Third World poverty in the first place.[16]

Ghana is an important case study particularly because of its long association with the two IFIs-the IMF and the World Bank. Throughout the 1980s and 1990s the country was a 'star pupil' for the neoliberal policies of these institutions.[17] But after more than two decades of faithful adherence to stabilization and adjustment policies of the BWIs, Ghana, like other African countries, remains highly indebted and poor.[18] In the mid-1990s Ghana was ranked 133 on the United Nations Human Development Index (HDI); in 2006 Ghana dropped to 136 after a marginal rise between 2002 and 2004. Almost half of Ghana's population lives in absolute poverty. Since the early 1990s, Ghana has emerged as one of Africa's new democracies and has, from 2001 onwards, been involved in the HIPC and the PRSP processes. The Ghana Poverty Reduction Strategy (GPRS), initiated in 2001 has been implemented since 2003 as the country's medium-term framework for poverty reduction. As a result, Ghana has benefited from much international assistance in the form of debt relief and increased bilateral and multi-lateral aid. Thus, the experience of Ghana as a leading reformer which has rigorously implemented the World Bank and the IMF's standard policy prescriptions since 1983 but has little to show in terms of sustained growth and poverty reduction, presents an interesting case for studying the impact of the recent policy shift by the IFIs.

This book is written within the context of the unequal and highly contentious process of neoliberal globalization.[19] This process, as argued by Mittelman, 'has become normalized as a dominant set of ideas and a policy framework.'[20] The book is an attempt to analyze and unpack mainstream representations and dominant narratives resulting from the neoliberal development discourse and to imagine alternative approaches. As argued by Sindzingre, poverty reduction emerged as the central focus of international development in the 1990s.[21] What

16 Smith, 2007.

17 Herbst, 1993; Boafo-Arther, 1999; Aryeetey, 2000.

18 Dzorgbo, 2001; Hutchful, 2002; Sachs, 2005:272.

19 My usage of globalization in this book follows that of other critical globalization scholars such James Mittelman (2000; 2004) who theorize globalization as encompassing 'an historical transformation in the interactions among market forces, political authority, and the lifeways embodied in society, as they encounter and join with local conditions' (see Mittelman, 2004:220).

20 Mittelman, 2000:4.

21 Zindzingre, 2004:165.

she has not however indicated is the reasons for this new consensus given that the same donors, for the preceding decade, as discussed in Chapter 3 in the case of Ghana, paid little heed to calls for 'adjustment with a human face.' This book, in part aims at filling this gap by tracing the evolution of the poverty reduction mantra within the international development discourse. How can we understand the global thinking of poverty over time and space? In other words, my work is interested in exploring the various ways that the so-called transition from the Washington to a post-Washington consensus has opened up spaces to both engage dominant paradigms of development and to imagine alternatives approaches for transformation and social change.

I draw on critical social theory, specifically Michel Foucault's notions of governmentality as a point of departure to theorize and unpack the new architecture of aid and its emphasis on country ownership through local participation. In order to understand the postcolonial development enterprise in Africa, and to analyze how this enterprise has been particularly shaped by the IFIs and neoliberal globalization, I deployed the concept of 'developmentality' as an analytical framework for my study.[22] My usage of *developmentality* refers to how postcolonial societies have been indirectly dominated and controlled by external forces through the use and mobilization of normative discourses such as 'development' and 'poverty reduction' with the tacit support of domestic social and political elites. Thus, since the attainment of political independence, the countries of Sub-Saharan Africa have been subjected to various forms of external intervention aimed at 'development.' This development imperative has meant that the continent has endured various theoretical positions, ideological competitions and policy experiments, sometimes with the support of governing elites. In the case of the poverty reduction discourse, I argue that through the use of words like 'participation,' 'ownership' and 'partnership,' the IFIs have been able to enlist the support of both governments and civil society groups behind what is largely a donor-driven agenda. In other words, *developmentality* enables us to think through the significance of the changing aid relations and to interrogate whether or not the new aid architecture departs from earlier paradigms. It explores the continuities of centralization of national development policy making, reinforced by the IFIs, and their mobilization, demobilization and selective exclusion of certain social groups. By critically exploring how the new poverty reduction discourse is phrased in the language of ownership and participation as a way of legitimizing the neoliberal agenda, my research aims to identify emerging trends in the politics of international development cooperation. While also locating my research within the broad theoretical framework of critical international political economy, my work also challenges the mainstream conceptualizations of power and the role of international financial institutions in constructing and promoting hegemonic ideas.

22 See Chapter 2 on how other Foucauldian scholars have used this term and an elaboration of my reformulation of the concept for my analysis of the new aid architecture.

My work also takes issue with some aspects of critical theory which posit that resistance to the neoliberal domination in the form of alternative perspectives on development are more likely to come from civil society.[23] Analysis of my field research and critical engagement with other aspects of critical social theory, including Foucauldian and postcolonial analysis, suggest the need for a more nuanced approach to understanding the role of civil society within policy spaces and political space more broadly. The emphasis of researchers and policy makers to date on the role of civil society within the poverty reduction framework has been on the involvement of civil society groups in policy formulation. Research and analysis have particularly focused on the formulation of poverty reduction strategy papers and the limitations of the 'stakeholder consultations.'[24] This existing work has therefore tended to focus on the changes for NGOs operating at a national level, although there is some discussion of how these organizations relate to civil society more broadly and at different levels. My research explores the multiple roles of CSOs in Ghana at different stages of policy process and at different levels, and examines the implications of the research in the context of the models implicit in the new architecture of aid. The study examines the challenges associated with the formulation and implementation of Ghana's Poverty Reduction process focusing on local participation and country ownership.

It is hoped that this book will stimulate further debate on the World Bank and IMF's new architecture of aid and result in improvements in the policy formulation process in aid recipient countries like Ghana. The book will contribute to the growing literature that focuses on changes to the international development architecture, especially within the context of Africa. As has been discussed in recent years,[25] a combination of events within the international political economy has fundamentally changed the aid and development architecture erected in the wake of the Thatcher-Reagan revolution of the late 1970s and early 1980s. While there are a number of studies which have examined the introduction of PRSPs within the African context, there are a few if any studies that explore questions around the politics of international aid relations from a Foucauldian and postcolonial perspective. My work therefore aims to contribute to the ongoing scholarly debate on the BWIs and their policies while exploring the relevance of the recent policy shift on development policy making as well as the long-term development agenda of postcolonial Africa.

23 Cox, 1999.

24 'Stakeholder consultations' have been used to describe the interaction between policy-makers, donors and civil society actors in relation to specific policies. As regards the poverty reduction strategy framework, this describes the consultation process among civil society representatives. See also, Godfrey and Sheehy, 2000; McGee et al., 2002; McGee and Norton, 2000.

25 Soederberg, 2004, Craig and Porter, 2006, Gould, 2006.

This book will also contribute to the growing literature on participatory development[26] by examining whether the emphasis on 'participation' within the poverty reduction framework has resulted in country-driven policy agenda and country-tailored policies. The study examines both the nature of participation and the governance strategies employed in relation to Ghana's poverty reduction process. As one of the first countries to have successfully implemented the neoliberal agenda of both economic and political reform, Ghana provides an excellent case for examining the 'new' aid and development architecture. Thus, this book offers a case study analysis of Ghana, one with conclusions that have relevance for Africa and other postcolonial societies.

The rest of the book is made up of five chapters. Chapter 2 establishes a distinct theoretical perspective inspired by the work of Michel Foucault and Postcolonial scholars such as Edward Said to re-think conventional analyses and interpretations of international relations and international political economy. In particular, this critical theoretical approach, which I call *developmentality*, offers a productive lens to show continuities and discontinuities in the global architecture of aid and to locate recent discourses on aid reform within the broader historical continuum of power inequalities in relation to international development cooperation and global governance generally. It also helps to problematize the self-disciplining effects of the new aid agenda. This theoretical framework helps to destabilize many of the binaries which have conventionally structured political thought: the domestic and international, the state and civil society, power and freedom, government and resistance. A variety of critical and post-colonial theorists are assembled to provide a theoretical tool-kit for analyzing the politics of the current aid regime. This framework gives structure to the analysis in subsequent chapters. Authors from African studies and critical development theory are introduced in order to show how African and other post-colonial societies are discursively constructed, produced and performed by recent discourses on good governance, poverty reduction, partnership, participation, ownership, and civil society. More importantly, this critical theoretical framework offers fresh approach to conceptualizing and analyzing power relations in the modern era; showing how power is increasingly de-centered and diffused at the international, national and local settings.

Chapter 3 provides a genealogy of the new architecture of aid in Africa by locating the changing international aid agenda within the more than a quarter of century neoliberal restructuring within the continent. Key texts such as the World Bank's 1981 Berg Report[27] are used to illustrate how Africa's post-colonies have been produced by specific Western discourses, policies, representations in order to justify and legitimize specific policy interventions. The chapter problematizes discourses such as the so-called 'African crisis'[28] and systematically chronicles

26 Nelson and Wright, 1995; Kothari et al., 2003; Giles and Mohan, 2004.

27 World Bank, 1981.

28 Leys, 1994; Arrighi, 2002.

and analyzes a combination of internal and external factors that resulted in a simultaneous curtailment of social provisioning of essential services that were central to the post-colonial social contract; and active introduction of market mechanisms of socio-economic governance in over 40 countries in Sub-Saharan Africa (SSA). Also discussed are the impacts of the implementation of the reform policies and the steady shift from the Washington to the so-called Washington Consensus policies.

The empirical analysis of the current aid regime represented by the poverty reduction framework begins in Chapter 4 with an exploration of Ghana's experience in implementing wide-ranging reforms since the launch of the economic recovery programs in 1983, effectively marking the end of the state-led development architecture of the post-independence era. The chapter traces the evolution of the recent poverty reduction policies to the implementation of their earlier structural adjustment policies and assesses the impact of these adjustment programs on Ghana's development process as an important context for the emergence of the poverty reduction agenda. In particular, the chapter highlights the social limits of neoliberalism in Ghana as reflected in the country's inability to bridge the rural–urban poverty profile and the withdrawal of the state from the provision of essential social services such as education and primary health care. In Ghana, and across much of Sub-Saharan Africa, neoliberalism is primarily associated with the one-size-fits-all macroeconomic policy prescriptions. Whatever the country, these prescriptions called for deregulation, currency devaluation, trade and financial liberalization, privatization of parastatals and reduction of public enterprises. In Ghana, for example, the commitment to privatization has led to user-fees in health and education, putting both public goods out of reach of large swaths of the population.

One of the claims made by conventional analysis on international aid agenda is the perceived avenues it provides for local participation in and ownership of development policy agenda. Chapter 5 explores this apparent shift towards inclusionary politics and active citizenship by drawing attention to the theatrical dimensions of the participatory methods of the poverty reduction strategy process. Focusing on civil society participation, this chapter seeks to answer the following questions: how is participation used by development and aid agencies? What are some of the ways 'civil society participation' has been theorized? How was participation used in the poverty reduction strategy process? These questions add to the overall aim of the manuscript, which is to critically examine the politics of participatory poverty reduction and development policy ownership. The chapter interrogates how different groups in civil society are involved and excluded in development policy making, and how such processes of inclusion and exclusion relate to citizenship rights, resource allocation and equity. The chapter also analyzes the seeming inconsistencies and contradictions embedded in the new architecture of aid in the realm of poverty reduction, ownership and empowerment; showing for example, how the new poverty reduction agenda while representing significant shifts from the rigid market fundamentalist policies of the Washington Consensus to emphasis on pro-poor and social policy, also represents new power dynamics in aid relations in the form of transformation of donor power and control exercised over aid recipient countries from top-down policy prescriptions to subtle, bottom-up donor-guided mechanisms; and the emergence of what I call 'elites consensus' comprising donors, political and civil elites.

The concluding chapter summarizes the book's main conclusions, by revisiting the question posed in the introduction on whether or not the new architecture of aid in the form of the poverty reduction agenda does indeed represent a rupture of Western development policy interventions in Africa and other postcolonial societies; or whether the new aid regime could be described to represent an emerging consensus between donors, political and social elites and influential NGOs who have deployed 'poverty reduction' as a new governing technology in order to reinforce unequal power relations and to re-impose neo-liberalism in Africa and other Postcolonial societies.

Chapter 2
Developmentality: A Postcolonial Perspective on the New Architecture of Aid

Introduction

This chapter introduces the theoretical framework for my analysis of the new architecture of aid being promoted by the International Financial Institutions (IFIs) in Africa and other regions of the global South. This new architecture of aid is represented by discourses around poverty reduction, local participation in, and ownership of development policy, development partnerships. My theoretical framework, which I call, *developmentality* frames this new architecture of aid, as a governing technology which not only reproduces Western constructions of Africa and other regions of the global South but also aims at legitimizing the re-imposition of neoliberal policies. The chapter begins with two samples of my interviews in Ghana as a backdrop for my theoretical framework and subsequent analysis. The chapter then explores Foucault's concept of governmentality, examining how it helps us to understand the operations of power in the modern era.

I arrived in Ghana on June 30, 2006 from my base in Canada to carry out field research on the implementation of the new aid agenda in Ghana. A few days after arrival, I launched myself into the task of interviewing and data collection on the evolution and implementation of the new poverty reduction discourse in Ghana. My first place of call was the Flagstaff House in Accra, the national capital. The Flagstaff House is considered a symbolic and historic national monument in view of the fact that the premises used to serve as residence and office for the country's first post-independence President, Osagyefo Kwame Nkrumah.[1] At the time of my visit, the heavily secured Flagstaff House served as offices for a number of government agencies and departments, including the National Development Planning Commission (NDPC). The NDPC is the key government agency responsible for coordinating all national development programs, including the Ghana Poverty Reduction Strategy (GPRS), the local version of the Poverty Reduction Strategy Papers (PRSPs). Once I introduced myself and provided information on the purpose of my visit, I was ushered into the office of a Senior Director who had agreed to answer all my questions. Below are excerpts from what transpired between us:

---

1 A new presidential office complex and residence, estimated at about $100,000 built and commissioned by former President John Kufuor in 2008 is located at the site of the former Flagstaff House.

Lord: Why did Ghana shift from the 'Economic Recovery Program' to the Ghana Poverty Reduction Strategy as a national development policy?

Officer: I won't accept the premise of your question … .there is no shift in policy … the GPRS is part of government policy aimed at overall national development … As we speak, we're working to launch GPRS 11 (Growth and Poverty Reduction Strategy) because the government believes there can't be poverty reduction without growth … we must first grow the economy then we can share …

Lord: Are you saying that the Ghana Poverty Reduction Strategy is different from the global poverty reduction discourse under the rubric of the World Bank and the IMF?

Officer: That's what I'm telling you … Ghana is a free and independent country and we implement our own policies. The World Bank and the IMF are our development partners … they don't tell us what to do …

Lord: I just want to be clear. Are you saying that all the reports about Ghana as one of the countries implementing a new set of donor policies are actually incorrect?

Officer: What am saying is the GPRS is not imposed on the country. We held a number of workshops here in Accra attended by Members of Parliament, Ministers and representatives from civil society and other stakeholders and also across the country attended by members of District Assemblies.

Lord: What about donors?

Officer: Of course they are our development partners and they have been invited to the workshops.

Lord: Is it not true, though that, donors do have the final say and could indeed veto the final product?

Officer: That's not correct … we work with our development partners and I'm sure disagreements over specific issues can always be worked out amicably. That does not mean donors have a final say … it's our own policy and that's what I want you to know.[2]

On August 8, 2006, while wrapping up on the second-leg of my field trip to Northern Ghana, I received an e-mail from the World Bank's Ghana office in Accra informing me about the availability of an economist from the local office to meet

2 Field Research Interviews in Ghana, July 4, 2006.

me in response to my earlier request for an interview. This was good news as I had almost given up on having an interview, especially as I was told only a couple of days earlier that all officials were on summer break and would not be back until September. It is Thursday August 10, 2006; 2.00pm local time and the venue is the plush World Bank office at Ridge Residential area in Accra:

> **Officer**: Good afternoon, Mr. Yevugah … or can I call you, Lord?
>
> **Lord**: Of course, call me Lord
>
> **Officer**: So you're doing your PhD in Canada … How long have you been there … Do you like it there … And do you know what you want to do when you're done … ?
>
> **Lord**: Yes, this is for my PhD dissertation … I have been working on it since September 2004 … No definite plans yet …
>
> **Officer**: Obviously you're a Ghanaian?
>
> **Lord**: Sure, I'm a proud Ghanaian and that brings me to my first question how long have you been with the Bank?
>
> **Officer**: Only for a couple of years …
>
> **Lord**: As an economist, what's your honest assessment of Ghana's economy?
>
> **Officer**: Well, honestly and between two Ghanaians, I would tell you Ghana is doing well … inflation is down, the Cedi [local currency] has been quite stable against the dollar and the government seems to be keeping its expenditure in check. In other words, all the prerequisites are there for a take-off and investor confidence in the economy has not been stronger …
>
> **Lord**: Sounds great … but haven't we been here before … talking about indicators and all … I mean what happened to all the promises of the Economic Recovery Program … Is not strange that after all these years of reforms we're still hoping for a 'take-off'?
>
> **Officer**: Well, as you know a combination of internal and external factors shape and influence the economy … take for instance, we spend so much on oil imports so any surge in oil prices in the world market automatically destabilizes the economy …

Lord: Exactly my point … we also continue to rely on export of few primary products … why can't we diversify the economy, add value or perhaps generate alternative sources of energy like wind, solar … .?

Officer: You're right, my brother … but as you well know, alternative sources of energy requires huge investment and time … I believe what is needed right now is to ensure that the fundamentals of the economy are sorted out first … and as I said earlier that's being done now …

Lord: And what's the role of the World Bank in all these … I mean, I guess you know about all the charges …

Officer: Well, the World Bank and other donors are partners and we only offer our expert advise … we don't meddle and we mean well for Ghana and our other partners. The World Bank has been involved in a number of projects aimed at poverty reduction and if you ask me I would say we're as committed to development and poverty reduction as the government and people of Ghana.

Lord: OK … well said, but how do you respond to those who accuse the Bank for being part of the problem rather than part of the solution … take for instance, the structural adjustment policies and how it has worsen poverty and caused much social hardships everywhere …

Officer: First, let me tell you, as a Ghanaian, I share your frustration and I am the first to admit there has been some failures but the World Bank listens and to tell you the truth, even me here talking to you is part of the transformation taking place at the Bank. A few years ago, you would have been talking with a British or American trained economist … a Whiteman … but here I am---Ghanaian, locally trained and very familiar with local issues and able to relate to peoples' everyday problems … I have family and friends as any other Ghanaian and you don't expect me to be involved with anything which will negatively impact my country … .

Lord: So are you saying that conditionality, top-down, donor driven and all the problems associated with the structural adjustment era are things of the past?

Officer: Definitely, the World Bank is not involved in the local policy-making process … we're invited as observers and experts … we don't make policies … that's for Ghanaian elected officials.

Lord: What about the accusation that the World Bank and other donors are the ones driving the agenda and that all the talk about local ownership and participation are cosmetic?

> **Officer**: If that's the case, then it is up to Ghanaian officials to speak out and protest ... as far as I know, the Bank works with Ghana's elected officials and we're very transparent about our dealings ... all our reports and agreements are online.[3]

The above and other 'encounters' in the form of interviews and my own analysis of data from other sources inform my theoretical framework which I will discuss in this chapter. Ghana, as indicated in the introductory chapter, offers an important case for studying the new international development agenda, one with conclusions that may have relevance for other countries in Africa and elsewhere in the global South. Contrary to the claim by donors that the new architecture of aid would place aid recipient countries in the driving seat of their own development agenda,[4] my analysis of data on Ghana shows a continuing donor involvement and limited role for government and societal actors. What is particularly disturbing is the fact that while Ghana's recent democratic credentials have been touted worldwide, the country's democratically elected officials including parliamentarians and members of District Assemblies are largely sidelined from the development policy making process.[5] Also, even though on paper[6] the Poverty Reduction Strategy Papers (PRSPs) are to be developed by citizens through open and public deliberations, my interviews and analysis of data reveal that 'local participation' in the process became synonymous with consultations with a selected group of technocrats, donors and urban-based and influential civil society organizations. While some of these findings confirm results of similar research undertaken elsewhere,[7] I have been really shocked about the attitudes of certain governmental and civil society officials (a case in point is my interview with the official at the NDPC) who seriously believe, and would stop at nothing to convince anybody who cares to listen, that countries like Ghana are indeed able to make their own development policies without interference from, and control by, any outside forces. It was largely the disconnect between the rhetoric of change in aid relations and the reality of continuity on the 'ground' coupled with what I saw as internalization of donors' rhetoric by political and civil elites which has led me to write this book with the view of engaging critically with the new aid and development agenda. Locating my study broadly

---

3 Field Research Interviews in Ghana, August 10, 2006.

4 World Bank and IMF, 1999.

5 Under Ghana's current democratic constitution, legislative power is exercised by parliament elected for a four year term. The country also has a decentralized administrative system whereby District Assemblies made of democratically elected members make laws for local administration as well discuss all proposed legislations to be introduced in the national parliament. See also *Constitution of the Republic of Ghana, 1992; Local Government Act (Act 462)*, 1993.

6 World Bank and IMF, 2002a; Klugman (ed.), 2002.

7 Ruckert, 2008; Gould et al., 2005. Fraser, 2005; Cheru, 2006; Stewart and Wang, 2006.

in the critical theoretical tradition, I have drawn and expanded on the concept of *developmentality* in order to develop my own theoretical approach for analyzing the exercise of power in postcolonial societies. The concept of *developmentality* has been used in recent times by different scholars from disparate academic backgrounds,[8] who like me have drawn on the work of Michel Foucault for their analysis. These scholars include Lynn Fendler whose work draws on Foucault's governmentality to frame developmental psychology, efficiency and behaviorism in education curricula as 'a technology of normalization.'[9] Thus, she argues, developmentality, like Foucault's governmentality, focuses on the self-governing effects of developmental discourse in curriculum debates: 'Developmentality, like governmentality, describes a current pattern in which the self disciplines the self.'[10] Also drawing on governmentality are Suzan Ilcan and Lynne Philips, who have deployed the concept of developmentality to frame development as 'a kind of mentality of government [that] carries with it technologies of rule which presume universal applicability.'[11] They also extend their analysis to what they call, 'global developmentalities [as constituting] a way to think about development politics on a global scale. It privileges a particular conception of knowledge and expertise as forces for social transformation. It elevates the status of certain professional experts as governmental authorities.'[12] Another usage of the concept of *developmentality* has been provided by Jon Harald Sande Lie who uses it specifically to analyze the new development architecture and poverty reduction strategies. Lie draws on Foucault's governmentality to analyze recent aid policies including the Comprehensive Development Framework (CDF) and the Poverty Reduction Strategy Paper (PRSP) framework. In particular, Lie's work delineates the participation–conditionality nexus of the recent aid policies and concludes that like governmentality, developmentality 'directs attention not only to the donor's coercive power and its transferral of knowledge, but also the policy objectives of good governance itself.'[13] The foregoing suggests a growing interest in Foucault's work in thinking through power relations and a range of policy interventions across different academic disciplines. My use of *developmentality* builds upon and, therefore, bears a striking resemblance to how it has been used by the others. My work, however, also offers an innovative application and usage of the concept, one which weaves together several strands of critical international theory and a range of complex empirical material. As well, my work initiates an important conversation between diverse academic disciplines such as international relations, development studies, postcolonial studies and African studies.

8 Fendler, 2001; Ilcan and Philips, 2006); Lie, 2005; 2008.
9 Fendler, 2001.
10 Fendler, 2001:120.
11 Ilcan & Phillips, 2006.
12 Ilcan and Phillips, 2006; 2007.
13 Lie, 2005; 2006; 2008.

My usage of *developmentality* suggests that understanding recent claims of transformation in aid relations in the form of the new poverty reduction paradigm requires analysis of power that departs from the ways in which conventional theories of international relations have analyzed and conceptualized power. Drawing on analyses of governmentality, as well as aspects of postcolonial theory,[14] I argue that the new international development agenda represented by poverty reduction discourse and related instruments which promise country ownership, participation and partnership, represent a technology of governance aimed at producing Africa and other regions of the global South as the poor, heavily indebted and uncivilized 'Other' of the modern, industrialized and the civilized West.[15] An examination of the evolution and implementation of the new aid agenda in Ghana and also its relationship to the New Partnership for Africa's Development (NEPAD),[16] suggests that framing these new policies in the language of ownership, participation and partnership has enabled African countries like Ghana to enroll in what is largely a donor-driven agenda. Unlike the period of colonialism where the emperor's power was exerted through brute force and repression, the power embedded in the present-day relations between Africa and the West is subtle or what Miller and Rose describe, 'governing at a distance.'[17] To govern at a distance, they argue, relates to 'indirect mechanisms of rule' such as techniques of notation, computation, surveys and mobilization of statistical data employed by the World Bank and the IMF to act upon individuals and whole populations.[18] The new aid agenda being promoted by the BWIs thus exemplify *governing at a distance*, with the emphasis on self-regulation or self-censorship. Thus by emphasizing country-ownership of, and participation in the poverty reduction strategy policy-making process while retaining the right to veto or reject the final product, the World Bank and the IMF are able to exercise a subtle control over aid recipient countries. As well, the emphasis on local ownership and participation excuses the two external institutions from accountability and puts onus on African governments who, in

14 In particular, my work draws on postcolonial scholars such as Said (1978); Mudimbe (1988); Ferguson (1994); Mazrui (1995); and Abrahamsen (2000); among others who have analyzed how, African was 'invented' produced and continued to be reinvented and reproduced as the 'Other' of the West through various discursive formulations, including 'development,' 'democracy' and 'good governance' etc.

15 For other works interrogating dominant constructs of Africa see Malinda S. Smith (2003; 2007).

16 The NEPAD was introduced by African leaders in 2001 with the support of Western donors as the new development blue-print of the continent. Among other things, the NEPAD initiative emphasizes trade, good governance and foreign directly investment as instrument for Africa's 'renaissance' (see Thabo Mbeki, 1998); see also http://en.wikipedia.org/wiki/African_Renaissance.

17 Miller and Rose, 1990:8; 2008.

18 Ohemeng, 2005.

turn suffer the consequences of public ridicule, delegitimization, civil unrest and electoral defeat.[19]

'Africa,' Mbembe argues, 'still constitutes one of the metaphors through which the West represents the origins of its own norms, develops a self-image, and integrates this image into the set of signifiers asserting what is supposed to be its identity.'[20] Analyses of the new multilateral aid agenda should therefore be situated within the context of the history of unequal power relations between Africa's aid recipient postcolonies and the Western donor institutions. Also, such analyses should be placed within the continuum of Western representations and (re)production of Africa[21] through discourses of development/underdevelopment also through the deployment of governing technologies such as self-regulation and consent which seek to enroll and implicate Africans in their own domination and discipline by the West. My theoretical framework, as indicated earlier in the chapter, weaves insights from the critical social theory of Michel Foucault, particularly his concept of governmentality as power/knowledge as well as discursive representations of Africa as articulated by postcolonial theorists such as Edward Said, Mahmood Mamdani, V.Y. Mudimbe, Rita Abrahamsen, Achille Mbembe and Ali Mazrui[22] among others to develop the concept of *developmentality*.[23] This concept is helpful in thinking through the new aid agenda and, specifically, the 'new' poverty reduction strategy discourse. It also helps to frame a question of this work, which is, how is the African postcolonial state governed?

The concept of *developmentality*, I argue, has been pivotal to the ways that Western countries and institutions have sought their legitimacy and thereby reproduce their domination over Africa's postcolonies. It involves the following different but interconnected representations: First, it involves how Africa and other regions of the global South have been discursively constructed by the West through colonial discourses and, in the postcolonial period through the discourse of development. This has not only resulted in a common sense imperativeness of 'development' in the postcolonial era but it has also resulted in the construction of colonial and postcolonial societies as the underdeveloped Other of the developed West. This construct, in turn, legitimized specific policy interventions.[24] It has also helped to deflect criticism against multilateral and bilateral donors for their policies as well as to delegitimize and marginalize alternative mechanisms for social change and development. Above all, *developmentality* also describes how,

19 Pender, 2007.

20 Mbembe, 2001:2; 2008.

21 Mudimbe,1988; Mazrui, 1995.

22 Said, 1978; Mamdani, 1996; Mudimbe, 1988; Abrahamsen, 2000; 2003; Mbembe; 2001; Mazrui, 2005.

23 My usage of 'developmentality' as indicated earlier in the chapter, builds on the works of others such as Lynn Fendler (2001); Suzan Ilcan and Lynne Philips (2006); John Harold Sande Lie (2005; 2008).

24 Duffield, 2007.

directly or indirectly, political and civic elites in Africa and other regions of the global South are implicated into accepting donor or externally driven policy prescriptions as common sense.[25]

The rest of the chapter is organized as follows: In the next section, I explore Foucault's concept of governmentality, examining how it helps us to understand the ways by which individual conduct is regulated in the modern era. Next, drawing on key postcolonial and critical development scholars who take Foucault as a point of departure, I explore how Africa and other regions of the global South have been discursively constructed by the West over the years from the colonial period to the present. In doing that, the chapter weaves together the work of Foucault and critical development theorists such as Christine Sylvester, Rita Abrahamsen, Uma Kothari among others who have explored the interconnections and divergence between development studies and postcolonial studies.[26] The final part of the chapter unpacks the 'new' architecture of aid, drawing on the contours of *developmentality* outlined earlier. The chapter concludes by suggesting that these policies not only reproduce Africa and other regions of the global South as the 'underdeveloped Other' of the West, but they also help to legitimize the (re) imposition of a neoliberal agenda.

Foucault, Neoliberal Governmentality, and Developmentality

As noted in the introduction to this book, for over three decades, Western countries and institutions have influenced and shaped the economic and development processes of countries in Sub-Saharan Africa and other regions of the global South. This dominance has been largely defined by the promotion of a neoliberal reform agenda. Drawing on classical liberalism and the ideas of scholars such as Adam Smith, David Ricardo and Milton Friedman, neoliberalism promotes and advocates unfettered liberalization of the economy and the belief in market forces, a non-interventionist state, minimal control on international economic interaction, individual freedom and responsibility.[27] Political liberalization and the emphasis on individual liberty and democracy have also been added in recent times within the rubric of good governance.[28] The promotion of these neoliberal ideas in the form of economic reform has been pivotal for global economic governance and North-South relations since the late 1970s and early 1980s.[29]

For Africa and other regions of the global South, the implementation of structural adjustment policies (SAPs) became not only the main instrument for mobilizing international aid but also these donor-driven policies became the basis

25 Taylor, 2006.

26 Sylvester, 1999; Abrahamsen, 2003; 2000; Kothari, 2001; 2002; Smith, 2003.

27 Cerny, 2008.

28 Abrahamsen, 2000.

29 Abrahamsen, 2004.

and the mechanism for national economic and development policy. In order to understand how this neoliberal agenda came to dominate Africa's postcolonial spaces and how it has reinvented itself over the years including the recent promotion of poverty reduction, country ownership and participation, requires innovative analysis of power which is distinct and departs from the conventional analysis. In recent years, various critical scholars have drawn on the work of Foucault to study power and governance in modern societies.[30] In particular, the concept of *neoliberal governmentality has been deployed to* extend Foucault's concept of governmentality in exploring and analyzing issues in contemporary global governance, particularly within the realm of neoliberal globalization.[31] These analyses frame neoliberalism as a new form of governing rationality which does not distinguish between state and market, or individual and market. Instead, state, society and individuals are perceived to function by the same logic as the market and can be understood by using economic models.

Thus, neoliberalism as a global governing rationality regulates the conduct of the aggregate population encompassed within the system of states, and that it addresses this key task by allocating responsibility for the government of specific populations to individual states, using treaties, trade and other devices to regulate the conduct of states, and promoting within states appropriate means of governing the populations under their control.[32] Thus, from a Foucauldian perspective, neoliberalism is a reinvention of classical liberalism where the emphasis on liberty, responsibility and empowerment become instruments of self-control and regulation. In other words, far from being a fundamentally disciplinary enterprise, as others like Stephen Gill have argued,[33] contemporary liberalism, according to the neoliberal governmentality school:

> combines its disciplinary focus with an emphasis on empowerment and self-government: the promotion of reforms designed to limit the freedom of action of governments, and therefore the ability of citizens to influence those actions, goes hand in hand with the promotion of democracy.[34]

While drawing partly on this literature for my own analysis of the recent multilateral aid agenda, I focus specifically on how this new form of governing rationality in the form of neoliberalism has uniquely different ramifications for postcolonial societies. The peculiar historical relations between these societies and the West in the form of colonialism and neocolonialism point to the conclusion

30 Peter Miller and Rose, 2008; Rose, 1999; Dean, 1999; Rose et al., 2006; Hindess, 2005; Barry et al., 1996; Burchell et al., 1999.

31 Abrahamsen, 2004; Mosse and Lewis, 2005; Ferguson and Gupta, 2002; Larner and Walters, 2004; Amoore and Langley, 2005; Lemke, 2001; Nadesan, 2008.

32 Larner et al., 2004:33.

33 Gill, 1995.

34 Larner et al., 2004:35.

that contemporary neoliberalism is a global governing rationality that is also racialized, resulting in the production if not the re-production of racial identities and subjectivities. Thus, while the new poverty reduction and related discourse could be described as a form of neoliberal governmentality, they also represent the reproduction of the historical representations of colonial and postcolonial societies as people in need of 'salvation,' 'civilization,' 'prosperity' and 'good governance.' In other words, while the Foucauldian perspective outlined above is helpful in thinking through aspects of contemporary neoliberalism, it is argued here that an analysis of the recent aid agenda in Africa and elsewhere in the global South will be incomplete without an integration of analysis of the effects of the power inequalities embedded in colonialism, colonial relations or what Scott calls, 'colonial governmentality.'[35] These unequal power relations, derived from racial representations of and domination over non-Western societies in the form of colonial occupation, have been reproduced in the postcolonial present in the form of what Nkrumah (1965) calls, 'neo-colonialism' and by extension, liberal and neoliberal interventions.[36] The power of the new donor-driven development and poverty reduction agenda stems from the way it represents Africa and other regions of the global South as in need of government, converting recipient countries into subjects of intervention and donors into their natural rulers. This new agenda therefore represents a continuum of Western representations of the South and thereby justifying the West's intervention in postcolonial societies.

In situating the analysis of the new aid agenda within the broader notions of power, Foucault's ideas of 'technologies of control' are invoked. In summarizing his own work, Foucault defines four major types of technologies that enter into the power games of truth:

> (1) technologies of production, which permit us to produce, transform or manipulate things; (2) technologies of sign systems, which permit us to use signs, meanings symbols, or significant; (3) technologies of power, which determine the conduct of individuals and submit them to certain ends or domination, an objectivizing of the subject; and (4) technologies of the self, which permit individuals to effect by their own means or with the help of others a certain number of operations on their own bodies and souls, thoughts, conduct, and the way of being, so as to transform themselves in order to attain a certain state of happiness, purity, wisdom, perfection, or immorality.[37]

While each of the four 'technologies' is important for understanding mechanisms of power, the analysis of the recent development and poverty reduction agenda focuses on the last two: 'technologies of power' and 'technologies of the self' which are central to domination of the development policy process of developing

35 Scott, 1995; Venn and Couze, 2006; Young, 2001.

36 Nkrumah, 1965: ix; see also Mawuko-Yevugah, 2010.

37 Foucault, et al. (eds), 1988: 18.

countries by the international financial institutions (IFIs). According to Foucault, it is the contact between the technologies of domination of others and those of the self (he calls) 'governmentality." In other words, by governmentality, Foucault sought to open up enquiry into the myriad of more or less calculated and systematic mechanisms and actions that seek to shape, regulate or manage the way people conduct themselves by acting upon their hopes, circumstances and environment.[38] Governmentality refers to the conduct of conduct, to steer and discipline people by working through their freedoms.[39] Here certain rationalities, or discursive fields, are thought to direct various techniques to be employed in order to work upon subjects' conduct. This has the consequence of disciplining people without their conscious recognition. These techniques work through discursive practices such as interactions between people, utilization of texts and symbols, education and surveillance in the form of audits and benchmarking that help constitute and reshape the subject's very identity so that its conduct gets moulded in order to suit specific purposes.[40] This form of power is particularly favored by a liberal climate as the 'conduct of conduct' depends on free subjects who then can be governed to act in certain ways but under the liberal banner of freedom.[41]

With his definition of governmentality, Foucault also introduced a new conception of power as productive and relational, and that draws attention to all the processes by which the conduct of a population is governed: by institutions and agencies, including the state; by discourse, norms and identities; and by self-regulation, techniques for disciplining and care of the self.[42] Crucially, the concept underscores how modern political power is exercised not simply by the state, but also by a multitude and network of actors, organizations and enterprises that seek to guide the behavior of individuals and their relation to things. It includes strategies, tactics and authorities—both state and non-state—that aspire to fashion the conduct of people both individually and collectively in connection to the economy and everyday life.[43] Also, it entails not only how the government governs the state, but also how individuals are supposed to govern themselves. Thus, the governor's direct rule is complemented with an indirect rule which is at this same time presented as liberal individualism—that humans get to feel a sense of freedom in governing themselves. My interview with the official at Ghana's National Development Planning Commission clearly illustrates this point: The official and others like him have assumed a false sense of freedom in drawing up their own national development policy when all the facts point to the contrary.

In his essay on governmentality, Foucault traces the genealogy of modern forms of power and notes that from the middle of sixteenth century until the end

38 Ferguson and Gupta, 2002.
39 Dean, 1999; also http://en.wikipedia.org/wiki/Governmentality.
40 Abrahamsen, 2004; Dean, 1999.
41 Hindess, 1996.
42 Foucault 1991:102.
43 Ferguson and Gupta, 2002.

of the eighteenth century, political writings shifted from a predominant concern with 'advice to the Prince/Ruler' to a concern with the 'art of government ... of how to be ruled, by whom, to what extent, and what methods, etc'.[44] According to Mitchell Dean, while the term 'government' is used as a more general term for any calculated direction of human conduct, the term governmentality seeks to distinguish the particular mentalities of arts and regimes of government and administration that have emerged since early modern Europe.[45] Foucault deploys the concept of governmentality as a guideline for the analysis he offers by way of historical reconstructions embracing a period starting from Ancient Greece through to modern neoliberalism. Mosse is thus right to argue that the recent changes in the aid architecture have produced new technologies of governance, which give attention to 'how programs enroll participants with the rhetoric of freedom, partnership, ownership or participation; how order or control is achieved through internalized disciplines of power.'[46] Thus an application of insights from governmentality is useful for deconstructing recent aid policies which, while promising autonomy for aid recipient countries have, in effect, strengthened the stranglehold of donors over the former's policy making space. As discussed in detail in Chapter 4, the introduction of the new aid agenda in Ghana has resulted in the introduction of a plethora of programs by the so-called development partners under the pretext of monitoring the efficiency of donor-sponsored programs and projects.[47]

According to Foucault, the dawning of governmentality and subsequent objectification of the human body resulted in other forms of power such as disciplinary power enacted by disciplinary technologies.[48] Within the human and social sciences, experts, professionals and specialists produced and promoted certain regimes of truth and acted as judges of normality.[49] Within these centralized administrative structures, a certain bio-power[50] emerged in which the human

---

44 Foucault, 1991:88, quoted by Olssen 2003.

45 Dean, 1999:2.

46 Mosse, 2005a:2.

47 These programs, which could be described as mechanisms of 'governing at a distance include policy forums, development dialogues etc. bringing together the so-called 'development partners' comprising representatives of donor governments and agencies, public officials and civil society organizations.

48 Foucault, 1977.

49 Rose, 1989; 1998.

50 In the *The Will To Knowledge*, his first volume of *The History of Sexuality (1998)* Foucault describes bio-power as the practice of modern states and their regulation of their subjects through 'an explosion of numerous and diverse techniques for achieving the subjugations of bodies and the control of populations.' Thus for Foucault, bio-power is a technology of power, which is a way of managing people as a group. In an era where power must be justified rationally, bio-power is utilized by an emphasis on the protection of life rather than the threat of death, on the regulation of the body, and the production of other technologies of power, such as the notion of sexuality. Regulation of customs, habits,

body became subject to observation and regulation, practiced in such institutions as prisons, hospitals and schools. Thus the aim of bio-power was to construct docile, obedient bodies to be subjected, used, transformed and thereby improved.[51] Contrary to Foucault's notion of sovereign power, by which power is hierarchical and plainly visible, disciplinary power is a form of power that is diffused: it is all encompassing, acting on everyone, and its constantly operating nature means that its effects are limitless. It acts swiftly and lightly, in such a subtle manner as to make it efficient, invisible and almost impossible to resist. Disciplinary power affects all aspects of individual and societal life, subjecting each and every person to constant surveillance.[52] Society and its individuals are therefore visible to and controlled by an impersonal and invisible disciplinary gaze. The application of this re-conceptualization of power is useful in thinking through the new aid mechanisms under the umbrella of the so-called new architecture of aid that makes government the responsible part of donor-driven policies as the government produced poverty reduction strategy. Like Foucault's Panopticon[53] which represented a form of disciplinary power,[54] the new aid architecture represents an emerging regime of surveillance and monitoring of the so-called heavily indebted countries. It represents a '... shift from the external controls of conditionality ... to the internal discipline of PRSPs and 'good governance' ... [which] has brought increased powers of surveillance and control over sovereign states, and more invasive monitoring of liberalization by IFIs.'[55]

Foucault's analysis of modern power in the form of governmentality also entails his discussion of the intrinsic relationship between power and knowledge. In particular, he identified the disciplinary potentials of knowledge and argued that knowledge is socially constructed and discursively produced in constructing subjectivities.[56] Foucault's socio-historical work on the discursive formation of sexuality and madness identified the ways in which knowledge became a productive force in defining these concepts and in disciplining, or governing,

health, reproductive practices, family, 'blood,' and 'well-being' would be straightforward examples of bio-power, as would any conception of the state as a 'body' and the use of state power as essential to its 'life' (See http://en.wikipedia.org/wiki/Biopower).

51 Lemke, 2001.

52 Covaleskie, 1993.

53 The Panopticon was an eighteenth century 'all-seeing' prison architectural and surveillance design aimed at ensuring that no prisoner could ever see the 'inspector' who conducted surveillance from the privileged central location within the radial configuration. The prisoner could never know when he was being surveilled. Foucault drew from the work of the British philosopher and legal theorist, Jeremy Bentham for his analysis of the transition from direct to indirect forms of power (see Foucault (1995) *Discipline and Punish,* pp. 195–228).

54 Foucault, 1977.

55 Mosse, 2005: 8.

56 Foucault, 1978.

social behavior to produce social difference.[57] Thus, a key aspect of Foucault's notion of governmentality, which I also find useful in the formulation of my own theoretical framework, is his conceptualization of knowledge as a discourse, and its relationship to power.[58] He defined discourse as durable propositions, or linguistic statements that have a semantic coherence within particular spaces that are practiced.[59] But rather than just words that represent, discourse forms objects and concepts by bounding how they can be thought of, talked about and acted upon. In other words, power relations are embedded in the ways we think of, speak about and relate to others. Thus, the institutionalization of discourse, or knowledge, as power is an important dimension of Foucault's work.

This new architecture of power by Foucault dramatically destabilizes conventional identification of power with domination. It provides a new understanding of power not as repressive or understood exclusively in material or institutional terms but as productive and creative of subjects.[60] Also, unlike social theorists who have argued that knowledge is defined by those holding economic and social power, Foucault introduced the idea of a sovereign concept of power to argue that power is an effect of and constituted by knowledge, and vice versa. Foucault rejected the premise that individuals wield power to control and impose their will. Instead, he reconceptualized the constructs of power and knowledge, as well as their relationship, to argue that power is a 'complex strategical situation',[61] that both produces knowledge as well as being in itself an effect of knowledge. In framing knowledge as situational, he emphasized the multiplicity of social relations (i.e. knowledge and mechanisms) that converge to enact knowledge. He interjected a spatial dimension in knowledge production as it was envisioned as an act, or practice, that is mobilized by a wide array of spatially dispersed and buttressing discursive and material relations. Foucault observed that the rise of the Enlightenment in the eighteenth and nineteenth centuries brought with it a new set of human sciences, such as Psychology and criminology. Already existing sciences underwent transformations, for example medicine, which changed from being a matter of classifying diseases to one that was anatomically based. The traditional humanist account of these changes suggests that they were a scientific and humane response to a set of pre-existing problems. Foucault's central thesis was that these sciences constituted discourses through which power was exercised over those classed as criminal, insane, or ill. Whereas humanism examined such discourses as progressive, humanitarian developments—the insane are now given medical treatment rather than being locked away—Foucault argued that the new sciences were a more efficient way of exercising power over target groups such as those classified as insane. Indeed, a crucial aspect of this exercise of power

57 Foucault, 1978; 1980.

58 Foucault, 1980b.

59 Foucault, 1972; 1979.

60 Dean, 1999; Abrahamsen, 2000; 2004.

61 Foucault, 1978:93.

was that these discourses actually created the problematic categories that they were supposed to deal with. Thus, criminology did not emerge in response to the problems associated with the activities of criminals and delinquents, but actually created those categories and begun to exercise control over the populace through classifying people into its various categories.

Postcolonial/Development Studies and Developmentality

Over the past few years, there has been a growing body of work within the field of critical development and postcolonial theory that analyze knowledge-power calculations embedded in development discourse and interventions in the global South.[62] With its ability to define 'others,' identify their 'problems,' and to legitimize 'professional' intervention in their daily lives, the field of development was subjected to critical analysis in the 1990s. Following Foucault, various critical development theorists have used the theoretical relationship between power and knowledge addressed by discourse analysis to attain 'a radical reading of subjectivity in the sense that through discourses individuals become subjects.'[63] In questioning the legitimacy of the developmental professional 'gaze'[64] to define and thus subjectify recipients of aid, critics of development have highlighted instead the importance of situated, local knowledge as opposed to the representational knowledge of professionals[65] but stressed that, all too often, it is the latter which, as 'legitimate' discourse, comes to shape interventions.[66] In exposing the co-evolution of 'the problematization of poverty' and 'development' with the growth, professionalization and institutionalization of expertise about the 'Third World,' Escobar reflects on the maintenance of such legitimation, as 'the result of the establishment of a set of relations among these elements, institutions, and practices and of the systematization of these relations to form a whole.'[67] While drawing broadly on this literature for my own analysis, my work is particularly informed by postcolonial scholarship. Following others like Gayatri Spivak, Homi Bhabha and Rita Abrahamsen,[68] my use of 'postcolonialism' refers to the persistence and continuity of colonial forms of power and domination in contemporary geopolitics of North-South relations. In other words, postcolonialism as used in my study seeks to map out new ways for thinking about techniques of power that define relations between the West and its non-Western 'Other.' Influenced by the work of

62 Ferguson, 1994; Escobar, 1995; Abrahamsen, 2000; 2004; Kothari, 2002; 2004.

63 Said, 1978, in Mohan, 1997.

64 Sachs, 1992.

65 Chambers et al., 1989.

66 Gardner and Lewis, 1996.

67 Escobar, 1995:40.

68 Spivak, 1988; Bhabha, 1994; Rita Abrahamsen, 2003.

Frantz Fanon, Kwame Nkrumah, Aimé Césaire[69] and other anti-colonial nationalist thinkers, postcolonial studies gained momentum in the 1970s with the publication of *Orientalism* (1978), one of the most influential works of Edward Said. Considered as one of, if not the most outstanding work within the postcolonial scholarship, *Orientalism*, marked a point of departure for examining European or Euro-American representations on non-Western peoples. This work draws largely on the general orientation for the discursive critique of representation provided by Foucault especially in *The History of Sexuality* and *Power/Knowledge.*[70]

According to Said, Orientalism is a 'systematic discipline by which European culture was able to manage, and even produce, the Orient politically, sociologically, militarily, ideologically, scientifically, and imaginatively during the post-Enlightenment period.'[71] Said's analysis is enriched by his incisive analysis of how the West had managed to establish an authoritative and an almost uncontested knowledge about the Orient and its peoples. This, as Abrahamsen argues, became 'a political vision whose structure promoted a binary opposition between the familiar and the strange.'[72] While the work of Said has been widely applied in literary and cultural studies, it is not until recently that there has been a growing body of work within the area of critical development studies which have applied his work to studies on discourses on development.[73] As argued by Abrahamsen, the reason for the attraction of Said's work to scholars and students of development studies is the growing conceptualization of development as a representational practice, whereby the 'Third World' and the 'poor' South is contrasted with, and juxtaposed against the 'developed' global North, similar to Said's 'Orient' vs. the 'Occident.'[74] Thus, for critical development theorists, the 'Third World' and 'development' are historical constructs, a particular way of seeing and acting upon the world that has less to do with the conditions it describes than with the constellation of social and political forces at the time of the emergence of the discourse. Key works in the area of development studies which have extensively drawn on aspects of postcolonial theory for analyzing various aspects of the theory and practice of development include James Ferguson's *Anti-Politics Machine*, Jonathan Crush's *Power of Development* and Arturo Escobar's *Encountering Development.*[75] These works provide the general framework for analyzing development as a discourse, i.e. as a Western form of social description. Analyses by critical development theorists have thus sought to disengage power relations embedded in development knowledge construction and development policy making. Consequently, a key objective of this literature has been to show how colonial projects of rule and

69 Fanon, 1965; 1968; Nkrumah, 1965; Césaire, 1968.

70 Foucault, 197; 1980.

71 Said, 1979:3.

72 Abrahamsen, 2003:200.

73 Abrahamsen, 2000.

74 Abrahamsen, 2000; see also Weber, 2004.

75 Ferguson, 1994; Crush, 1995; Escobar, 1995.

the postcolonial project of 'development' have defined differential modes of citizenship, and, in the process, enacted what Foucault termed subjectivation, a 'mode of objectification which transform[s] human beings into subjects.'[76]

Abrahamsen has noted that a common thread which links various strands of postcolonialism is 'a deep engagement with the role of power in the formation of identity and subjectivity and the relationship between knowledge and political practices.'[77] This commonality of interrogation of power, she argues, is perhaps, a clear indication of postcolonialism's relationship and indebtedness to poststructuralist and postmodernist thinkers, which in my view include Michel Foucault. Adopting Foucault's emphasis on the discursive practices of subjectivation, postcolonial scholars such as Valentine Y. Mudimbe and Mahmood Mamdani have analyzed the creation of categories of race, gender and ethnicity by the West as a project of domination, and have sought to show how various representations serve the purpose of objectification of subjects.[78] As argued by Chowdhry,[79] the focus of postcolonial analysis on several factors provides us with a unique vantage point from which to examine power in the postcolonial world. These factors, as she argues include: first, the colonial project as foundation in shaping the modern world; second, the salience of representation through narratives of race, gender, class, and nation; third, the silences and erasures of international relations and around race (and its intersections) despite its foundational presence in global politics; fourth, the centrality of global capital in the construction of the modern world; and fifth, the importance of resistance and agency. For postcolonial scholars like Chandra[80] the prevailing social, economic and political situation in the postcolonial world has an intrinsic relationship to the colonial past.

A postcolonial approach to aid reform and development shifts the terrain of enquiry from universal versus cultural relativism debate to one premised on an enquiry into the operations of power relation to knowledge formation. Thus the importance of the imperial project to knowledge production about colonized cultures is noteworthy. Equally important to note are the continuities and disjunctures in knowledge production that came about as a result of decolonization and that are emerging in the context of neoliberal globalization today. In other words, narratives of development and poverty reduction must be situated within the colonial and postcolonial discursive political economy of hierarchy and representation, and postcolonial analysis of poverty reduction must come to terms with discourses of development, identity production and power by asking how are the ideas about development are constructed? What representations and identities do they enable? How are the global and local capital implicated in the discourses on development, poverty and poverty reduction?

76 Foucault, 1983:208.

77 Abrahamsen, 2003:197.

78 Mudimbe, 1988; Mamdani, 1996; see also Moore, 2001 for a review.

79 Chowdhry, 2004.

80 Cited in Kothari, 2002.

In *Orientalism*, Said argues that the 'Orient,' which essentially includes every non-Western society, has been systematically managed and even produced, by the literature and knowledge created and circulated by the latter pertaining to the former.[81] He demonstrates that Western-based literature on the 'Orient' is a manifestation of unequal power relations in regards to who can deem what is truth on any given subject.[82] Further, he asserts that the knowledge that has been created is rife with self-congratulation, rendering anything that is deemed to be 'Other' as possessing all of the characteristics which are asymmetrical to those believed to exist in Western societies.[83] Other Africanists, including Mudimbe and Mazrui[84] have drawn and expanded on the work by Said to explain what Mudimbe describes as 'alterity'[85] or the '(re)invention'[86] of Africa as the 'Other' to the West. Thus, a powerful dichotomy is produced which portrays the West as exhibiting all that is good, normal, advanced, and rational, and the 'Other' is inherently depicted as the embodiment of the antonyms of the aforementioned virtues. The ultimate expression of power in regards to knowledge construction is manifested when these ideas acquire authority and are considered normal and uncontested truths.[87] Building on Said's work, Mudimbe and Mazrui have argued that this 'Otherness' of Africa in relation to the West is very central to the very idea of invention and re-invention of Africa in the Western imaginary including representations in the media, popular culture and particularly in recent discourses on good governance and development.[88] In this regard, as argued by Kothari[89] the origins of the field of development studies, and the resulting Eurocentric forms of knowledge that it produces, can be partly situated in the colonial moment and thus the technologies and approaches embodied in, and articulated by, development emerge from specific times and places. And the 'disciplinary after-effects' of colonization could not be captured better by Said:

> To have been colonized was a fate with lasting, indeed grotesquely unfair results, especially after national independence had been achieved. Poverty, dependency, underdevelopment, various pathologies of power and corruption, plus of course notable achievements in war, literacy, economic development: this mix of characteristics designated the colonized people who had freed themselves on one level but who had remained victims of their past on another.[90]

81 Said, 1979.
82 Said, 296.
83 Said, 296
84 Mudimbe, 1988; Mazrui, 2005
85 Mudimbe, 1988 (cited by Smith 2006:3).
86 See Mazrui, 2005.
87 Mazrui, 325.
88 Smith, 2006; see also Abrahamsen, 2000.
89 Kothari, 2002.
90 Said, 1989: 207.

In *Encountering Development*, Escobar drew on the works of both Foucault and Said to analyze the relationships between power and knowledge in the discursive construction of the Third World through the discourse of development. He examined the way in which, through the ensemble of relations between institutions, powerful ideas, modes of authority and techniques of information and surveillance, the description of problems and prescription of solutions through development discourse were determined not by 'the objects with which it dealt but by a set of relations and a discursive practice that systematically produced interrelated objects, concepts, theories, strategies.'[91] Escobar argues that the very idea that there existed 'developing' and 'developed' countries, and a 'Third World' which was 'underdeveloped,' was the product of the Western regime of order and truth reflected in an objectivist and empiricist stand that dictates that the Third World and its people exist 'out there,' to be known through theories and intervened upon from the outside. Focusing on development interventions in parts of Latin America, Escobar argues that the Euro-centric model of development has entrenched itself so completely that alternative perspectives of development are difficult—if not impossible, to imagine.[92] Escobar further elaborates on Said's ideas, by asserting that 'development' is not natural, but rather a 'historical construct in which "poor" countries are known, specified, and intervened upon' by the West.[93] Viewed in this light, the post-Second World War development project is not a failure, but rather a complete success in its effective management of the global South.[94] Thus, according to Escobar, development is a business or enterprise which has exercised its discursive power to manufacture what we now consider 'developed' and all its antonyms. The implications this has on development policies and projects is that 'development' is reduced to the experiences of what are considered 'developed countries' within the hegemonic discourse, vis-à-vis industrialization, modernization, privatization and liberalization, etc.[95] Norman Girvan reasserts Escobar's arguments, stating that 'power imbalances in knowledge are expressed in the global North's dominance in knowledge construction, reproduction and dissemination.'[96] He argues that although there are many mechanisms to control people, the greatest is knowledge because of its 'ability to condition routine behavior without resorting to physical force or material sanction.'[97] Essentially, by controlling what people know, those who control the construction of knowledge can determine 'the conditions that people believe to be necessary, desirable, possible, and acceptable.'[98]Also, the reasons

91 Escobar, 1995:42.
92 Escobar, 1995:383.
93 Escobar, 1995:384.
94 Escobar, 1995.
95 Escobar, 1995:383.
96 Girven, 2007:7.
97 Girven, 2007:7.
98 Girven, 2007: 8.

for the West's unrivalled ability to produce what is enshrined as development knowledge is 'the size of their budgets, number of professional staff, access to the best and brightest researchers, technology infrastructure, size of libraries and data bases, privileged access to the centers of political and financial power, access to information, and ability to carry out comparative cross-country research and advisory functions.'[99] In sum, the West is able to dominate and control the construction of development knowledge because of its ability to take advantage of the outlets provided by globalization. Development as an invention has also been explored by other scholars. Wolfgang Sachs argues that the Third World was created in the post-WWII era as United States President Harry S. Truman, through his 'Point Four Program' (or Bold New Program), which called for increased aid to developing countries, equated underdevelopment with a lack of economic growth.[100] Inadvertently, along with the creation of the 'Third World' came notions of catch-up theories of development which called for a mimicking of the West on the part of the underdeveloped countries. Other scholars have explored the repercussions of the existence of hegemony within development knowledge. Suzanne Soederberg argues that development knowledge is limited because of the hegemony of global capitalism as a world organizational system.[101] She argues that in this light, development is only imaginable through some form of economic relationship with the global North, as normally facilitated through the IFIs. The inherent problem with this structure is that the hegemonic North has a vested interest in maintaining that position, and thus any development policies it produces or supports will not have the interests of the developing countries as its ultimate goal. Thus, because the goals of the global North and the global South are inherently asymmetrical, development policies and knowledge will always be produced in a way that administers to the desires of the global North over the global South. Similarly, Heloise Weber demonstrates how the discourse of development is imbued with power because of the role of geopolitics.[102] She argues that hand in hand with development are notions of developing states in the Third World and developed states of the North with the latter always devising strategies of reproducing their influence and domination over the former.[103] She interprets contemporary international development strategies being promoted by Western donors as an attempt not only to reconstitute the political utility of the Third World, but also as means of reproducing the politics of global inequality. Also relevant for my analysis of the new aid agenda and in imagining avenues for resistance and emancipation is the work by those in subaltern studies. In 'Can the Subaltern Speak?,' Gaytri Chakraborty Spivak asks if the underprivileged groups in the global South including women and other racial minorities have

99 Girven, 2007:20.
100 Sachs, 1992.
101 Soederberg, 2004.
102 Weber, 2004:188.
103 Weber, 2004:188.

the agency required not only to express themselves but to be heard given their subordinate positions of power.[104] While acknowledging the restrictions and 'road-blocs' confronted by the subaltern, she admonishes the postcolonial critic to take account of these road-blocs and find ways to break the dominance of imperial and hegemonic ideas. It is my view that countries in Africa and other regions of the global South do have the capacity and potential for agency and resistance in this historical moment where ideas of neoliberal globalization have become dominant and entrenched.

New Architecture of Aid and Biopower

That the new architecture of aid in the form of the poverty reduction discourse constitutes a new biopower is a point eloquently articulated by Tan (2011). According to her:

> the PRSP project not only reframes fundamental tenets of international co-operation and global communal responsibility but also establishes a new disciplinary framework for Third World state engagement with the global economy and the international law which sustains it. In this way the discourse and methods of resistance against the injustices of the international order have been appropriated to distil such dissent through qualified operationalising of contestable notions of "participation," "ownership," "partnership" and "poverty reduction."[105]

Such a conclusion coheres with my own analysis of the new architecture of aid as part of a new set of technologies which reproduces Western representations of Africa and other regions of the global South in ways that legitimize their intervention in these regions. This entails the introduction of a series of governing techniques aimed at self-regulating and disciplining populations of the South by themselves or what I call developmentality. The concept of developmentality as explained earlier helps us to analyze these new forms of regulation as well as theorize IFIs as agents of neocolonial intervention. Such an analysis offers a more compelling understanding of the new poverty reduction discourse as one that is imbued with power by synthesizing Foucault's notion of govermentality and disciplinary power with the postcolonial interpretations of the intrinsic unequal power relations between the global North and South, manifested in ideas on, and about development. In other words, analysis of contemporary international aid policies must be situated within the colonial and postcolonial discursive constructions of Africa and other regions of the global South, particularly in relation to narratives and discourses about development. Foucault's concept of biopower is

104 Spivak, 1988.

105 Tan, 2011:1039.

also useful in understanding the racialized aspect of recent aid policies. Distinctly different from both sovereign power and disciplinary power, biopower, according to Foucault, targets the life of a population.[106] Thus by seeking to impose a certain way of life on a people in the form of aid policies and given that these policies are mainly applicable to particular countries and in certain regions of the world presupposes and reproduces Western superiority. Such a development would also represent a throw-back of what is described earlier as former US president Truman's 1949 Orientalist representations of nations of the southern hemisphere as poor and in need of US, and by extension Western, benevolence.[107]

Also, it is important to recognize how agents of neoliberalism have sought their domination in the postcolonial world through consent and by enlisting the support of political and societal elites. The acceptance and adoption of recent poverty reduction policies by the global South represents a different form of power relations in which the former colonies (which now constitute the global South) consensually adopt the 'systems' that are promoted and dominated by agents of neoliberal hegemony. The nature of the new aid relations, while maintaining unequal power relation, has relied less on brute force and coercion and more on consent, to the extent that African governments, instead of resisting and opposing the new development policies and interventions as being Eurocentric or neocolonial and racist, has embraced these policies and called them their own. A typical example here is the New Economic Partnership for African Development (NEPAD) which emerged towards the end of 1990s as Africa's own home-grown response to the challenges of development.[108] A biopolitical developmentalist perspective, initiatives such as NEPAD are meant to integrate Africa and other regions of the global South into what is largely Western-dominated global economic governance agenda that seeks to perpetuate a neoliberal hegemonic agenda. Thus, by adopting and accepting initiatives such as HIPC, NEPAD, and the PRSPs, Africa and other regions of the global South have accepted not only their categorization as 'poor' but have also consensually allowed the agents of neoliberal globalization to define what constitutes appropriate form of 'development' and what types of institutional mechanism are able to bring it about. The fact that the global South has internalized the knowledge produced by the global North in regards to development knowledge demonstrates just how entrenched power relations are in knowledge construction. Development theory as well as policies promoted in the global South should be understood as a form of 'technology' and 'control' which seek to frame aid recipient countries in a particular image that make it easy for them to be dominated by powerful countries and institutions which seek to impose a particular set of social, economic and political policies and world views.

Under the new architecture of aid, countries which have opted for the IMF and World Bank's HIPC initiative are expected to formulate a country's PRSP,

---

106 Foucault, 2003.

107 Escobar, 1995:3.

108 Abrahamsen, 2004.

showing how the money accruing from debt relief would be utilized for 'poverty reduction.'[109] This seeming paradigmatic shift in the international aid architecture in the form of transition from donor-led structural adjustment policies to country driven poverty reduction strategies, suggests that aid recipient countries are now in the position to determine their own development agenda. I argue however that, as the PRSP needs World Bank/IMF approval to become operational, this inclines the government to produce a document that reflects donors' policies in order to release funding, which the government, in the case of Ghana and others in Africa, is highly dependent upon. And as a result of other new mechanisms such as what is called aid harmonization and budgetary support, the so-called donors, are able to exercise even greater control over the development policy agenda of their developing country clients. The poverty reduction framework effectively entails a process aimed at making the donors' conditionality, policy and objectives those of the recipients, thus the arrangement of donor–recipient relationships comprises an indirect exercise of power.[110] This, without doubt, is akin to power/knowledge linkage as illuminated by Foucault in his other later works. The recent donor policies which seek to alter power relations between donors and aid recipients have had the effect of not only reproducing donors power but more significantly these new aid policies have introduced new rationalities of governance.

The discussion on governmentality shows how exercise of modern forms of power have entailed the 'conduct of conduct' which, according to Fouacult, draws on the idea of collective mentalities indicating that individuals govern themselves because they have internalized the governor's mentality.[111] In relation to the new architecture of aid therefore, the application of governmentality helps us to deconstruct specific claims made by donors. In particular, my study suggests that, as a way of staving off criticism of their SAPs, the IFIs have introduced a new set of governing strategies that are fundamentally neoliberal in character and which encourage the continuing domination of the development agenda of poor countries. For instance, through the new framework of the consultative processes in the formulation of poverty reduction strategy papers, formal democratic institutions in countries like Ghana have been sidelined in the policy making process, resulting in a reconfiguration of the relationship between the state, NGOs, and foreign aid donors.

Operating at both formal and informal levels of social and political interaction, this new mentality of government employs coercive and co-optive measures to cultivate local participation in the neoliberal modernization project, while continuing to neglect the longstanding unequal trade relations between developed and developing countries. As will be demonstrated in the analysis of my field data on the poverty reduction strategy process in Ghana, the role of NGOs and consultants engaged in the new aid agenda is to merely use civil society to

109 IMF and World Bank, 1999; Thomas, 2004.

110 Lie, 2005; 2006.

111 Dean, 1999.

legitimize the neoliberal project. In view of the fact that government officials and civil society organization are largely powerless in influencing the content of these country strategy papers and the fact that the IFIs have the final say on whether or not the final document is acceptable, the poverty reduction papers represent a governing technology that reinforces the persistance of neoliberalism as the new form of Western hegemony and influence in Africa's postcolonies. It is within this context that development theory, as well as policies promoted in Africa and other regions of the global South, can be understood as a form of governing technology which seeks to frame aid recipient countries in a particular image that makes it easy for them to be dominated by powerful countries and agents who seek to impose a particular set of social, economic and political world view. Such analysis coheres with that of other critical scholars who have deployed a Foucauldian analytical lens to explore changes in the world economy especially in an era of unbridled neoliberal globalization.[112] These scholars have interpreted the seeming shift towards post-Washington Consensus policies in the form of new aid-related reform packages as representing a productive power which is aimed at regulating individual conduct. It comprises relations of power where the governor seeks to let individuals govern themselves after they have internalized the mentality dispersed by the governor, aiming to guide and shape actions of others or oneself.[113]

Within the context of international aid relationships, there is a clear deployment of such techniques by the IFIs. Specifically, the new aid agenda with emphasis on country ownership/participation could be seen as part of a wide-range of neoliberal sponsored technologies designed to produce self-governing subjects.[114] When studying the evolution of neoliberal principles of government in the works of Hayek and Chicago School Economists such as Friedman, Foucault and subsequent governmentality scholars argue that neoliberalism as a body of knowledge, strategies, and practices of government seeks to divest the state of paternalistic responsibility by shifting social, political and economic 'responsibility' to privatized institutions and economically rationalized 'self governing' individuals. Thomas Lemke's work illustrates how the state attempts to divest itself of 'responsibility' for its citizens by recasting them as rational, self-responsible/choosing agents:

> The neoliberal forms of government feature not only as direct intervention by means of empowered and specialized apparatuses, but also characteristically develop indirect techniques for leading and controlling individuals without the same time being responsible for them. The strategy of rendering individual subjects "responsible" (and also collectives, such as families, associations, etc.) entails shifting the responsibility for social risks such as illness, unemployment, poverty, etc. and for life in society into domain for which the individual is

112 Rose, 2000; Ferguson and Gupta, 2002; Mosse, 2005.

113 Cruikshank, 1999.

114 Rose, 2000.

> responsible and transforming it into a problem of "self-care." The key feature of the neoliberal rationality is the congruence it endeavors to achieve between a responsible and moral individual and economic rational individual.[115]

Thus, by stressing 'self-care,' the neoliberal state divulges paternalistic responsibility for its subjects but simultaneously holds its subjects responsible for self-government.[116] These ideas, I argue, are applicable within the context of international development cooperation where a multitude of transnational actors have applied a neoliberal governmentality as a strategy 'to govern at a distance.'[117] As subsequent chapters will show, the aid agenda, apart from reproducing Western representations of Africa and other regions of the global South in ways that legitimize their intervention in these regions, has also entailed a series of governing techniques aimed self-regulating and disciplining populations of the South by themselves.

Summary and Conclusion

This chapter has sought to develop a theoretical framework that will help to think through the new multilateral aid and development as a form of a new rationality of governance. It explored the critical literature that interrogates how Africa and other regions of the global South have been framed through the 'invention' of development by the West in order to define the South as the 'Other.' Drawing on aspects of the work of Foucault and aspects of postcolonial theory, the chapter expanded on the concept of *developmentality*, which I suggest, provides an innovative theoretical framework that seeks to situate the new aid agenda being spearheaded by the IFIs within the context of unequal power relations between 'partners' in international development community made of donors, governments in Africa and across the global South and civil society organizations. This critical theoretical framework helps us to understand how the postcolonial African development agenda continues to be dominated and shaped by a Western development paradigm promoted by IFIs and the neoliberal agenda. It also shows how the new aid agenda represented poverty reduction framework reinforces the undue influence of IFIs on African countries like Ghana, undermines their democratic processes and threatens their sovereignty by inscribing the externally-driven and dominated neoliberal policy agenda.

---

115 Lemke, 2001.

116 Nadesan, 2008.

117 Miller and Rose, 1990; 2008.

Chapter 3
Africa and the New Politics of International Development Cooperation

Introduction

By the mid to late 1980s, barely two decades after decolonization on much of the African continent, a new development orthodoxy—which came to be known as structural adjustment policies—had become the main instrument for development policy making. How did this become the case? And what were the implications of this new agenda for Africa's development process? This chapter explores the rise, evolution and application of this neoliberal development agenda in Africa. Through the lens of *developmentality*, the chapter argues that since the early 1980s, this agenda has come to represent a reproduction of policy mechanisms designed to police and regulate the postcolonial state. The chapter first provides a brief overview of what came to be known as the 'African crisis'[1] arguing that this crisis, which came to be conceptualized as the 'failure of development'[2] has its internal and external origins. In order to understand how this crisis evolved it is important to understand the competing ideological orientations which have influenced Africa's postcolonial development process.

The chapter will provide a general overview of how 'development' became the rallying point for both the first generation of African leaders in the postcolonial era as well as external bodies that also invoked development as a strategy to maintain their influence in the post-colonies. I will then historicize discussion about the 'African crisis' and the competing policy prescriptions to solve this problem by African leaders on one hand, and the IFIs on the other. The chapter will then offer a genealogy of the neoliberal agenda in African to the publication of the Berg Report in 1981 and explore how this coincided with key developments within the global economy. The main thrust of this chapter is to show how, as a result of a combination of internal and external factors, the two BWIs have been able to establish their hegemony in postcolonial Africa. The introduction of neoliberal policy prescriptions in African countries represents a reimposition of Western domination on Africa's postcolonial countries. Thus, the chapter will show that the postcolonial moment is characterized by 'developmentality' whereby the population is governed through the use of the discourse of development. The recent shift to PRSPs is a part of this genealogy. The chapter will also explore

1 Leys, 1994; Giovanni Arrighi, 2002.
2 Ahluwalia, 2001.

the emergence of the new aid and development architecture in the form of a global consensus towards poverty reduction. It will trace the emergence of this new consensus to the disastrous implementation of SAPs. It then explores the transition from SAPs to PRSPs, by mapping out what is new in PRSPs, and what persists. I will provide a discussion of the shift from the Washington Consensus to the Post-Washington Consensus in the form of the World Bank's Comprehensive Development Framework and incorporation of social development into future bilateral and multilateral lending arrangements. I will argue that the new poverty reduction discourse represents, more or less, a reinvention of the neoliberal development agenda promoted by the BWIs -rather than a new global consensus—one that is more inclusive and departure from the neoliberal policies of the past few decades.

Postcolonial Africa and the 'Crisis' of Development

By the early 1960s, the majority of African countries had attained political independence and the status of sovereignty, thus ushering in a new era of not only state formation and state-society relationships, but more significantly, the construction of a new form of relations between the newly independent countries and the international community including the ex-colonial powers. According to Ake,[3] independence had re-positioned former colonial states to rally around the idea of development in order to maintain their presence and some leverage in the former colonies and to gain allies in the battle against communism. Thus, the ideology of development became 'a strategy of power that merely capitalized on the objective need for development.'[4] This postcolonial obsession with 'development' partly describes what I call *developmentality* or the exploitation of the ideology of development as a means of reproducing political and economic hegemony in the postcolonial era without any serious commitment to the transformation of the colonial state and the economy. This '*develop-mentality*' during the early postcolonial era was manifested in competing ideas advanced by African leaders and external bodies like the World Bank on how best to advance 'development.' Drawing on ideas espoused by dependency theorists,[5] a number of first generation African leaders led by Ghana's founding President, Kwame Nkrumah sought to steer their newly independent countries away from what was described as

3 Ake, 1996.

4 Ake, 1996:9.

5 Dependency theorists such as Frank (1971); Wallerstein (1975); and Amin (1976) have identified the obstacles to Global South development in structural differences between production and trade in the North and the South rooted in colonial history; and that the present arrangements in the international economy have ensured that countries of the North develop at the expense of those in the South.

'neo-colonialism.'[6] In *Neo-Colonialism: the Last Stage of Imperialism* (1965), Nkrumah argues that, although countries like Ghana had achieved political independence, the ex-colonial powers and newly emerging superpowers such as the United States continued to play a decisive role in their cultures and economies through new instruments of indirect control such as international monetary bodies and multinational corporations.[7] According to Nkrumah,

> Neocolonialism is ... the worst form of imperialism. For those who practice it, it means power without responsibility and for those who suffer from it, it means exploitation without redress. In the days of old-fashioned colonialism, the imperial power had at least to explain and justify at home the actions it was taking abroad. In the colony those who served the ruling imperial power could at least look to its protection against any violent move by their opponents. With neo-colonialism neither is the case.[8]

For Nkrumah, the only viable means by which postcolonial African countries could secure and safeguard their newly independent states was to unite not only through the formation of a continental government but also to chart a path of non-align relationships with global powers.[9] Through a series of conferences and writings, he fiercely promoted these ideas across Africa.[10] All this culminated in the formation of the Organization African Unity (OAU) in 1963. Thus, in many ways, the formation of the OAU as a continental body and platform for espousing pan-African ideas and solutions to African problems owed much to the vision and charisma of Nkrumah. The OAU until its replacement by the African Union in 2001 came to embrace the dependency approach that blamed the continent's underdevelopment on external factors.[11]

Since the attainment of independence, Barbara Grosh, argued virtually every sub-Saharan African country has pursued state-led policies ranging from

---

6 In the introduction to *Neo-colonialism: The Last Stage of Imperialism*, Nkrumah states: the essence of neo-colonialism is that the State which is subject to it is, in theory, independent and has all the outward trappings of international sovereignty. In reality its economic system and thus its political policy is directed from outside.

7 Ashcroft, 2000; Benjamin, 2007.

8 Nkrumah, 1965:xi.

9 Nkrumah was a founding member of the Non-Aligned Movement (NAM) which resulted from the 'Bandung Conference' of Third World leaders held in Bandung, Indonesia, in 1955.

10 Apart from declaring on the day of Ghana's independence (March 6, 1957) that 'the independence of Ghana was meaningless unless it is linked with the total liberation of Africa,' Nkrumah also hosted a series of pan-Africanist conferences in Ghana and provided both material and moral support to countries still under colonial rule. See also his book, *Africa Must Unite* (1963), for his views on the imperative and urgency of African unity.

11 Owusu, 2006.

substantial regulation to control by planners.[12] External forces like the World Bank and IMF on the other hand, believed that for postcolonial Africa to 'catch up' with the rest of the world in terms of development and industrialization, it had to embrace strategies promoted by modernization theorists.[13] Not only did these competing ideologies provide the basis for development policy making in the postcolonial era, but more significantly, they also provided the framework for diagnosing and sorting out what came to be known variously as the 'African crisis' or the 'African tragedy.'[14]

The nature and scope of the 'African crisis' was summarized by Giovanni Arrighi as follows:

> In 1975, the regional GNP per capita of Sub-Saharan Africa stood at 17.6 percent of 'world' per capita GNP; by 1999 it had dropped to 10.5 percent. Relative to overall Third World trends, Sub-Saharan health, mortality and adult-literacy levels have deteriorated at comparable rates. Life expectancy at birth now stands at 49 years, and 34 percent of the region's population is classified as undernourished. African infant-mortality rates were 107 per 1,000 live births in 1999, compared to 69 for South Asia and 32 for Latin America. Nearly 9 percent of Sub-Saharan 15 to 49-year-olds are living with HIV/AIDS—a figure that soars above those of other regions. Tuberculosis cases stand at 121 per 100,000 people; respective figures for South Asia and Latin America are 98 and 45.[15]

While there have been disagreements among Africanists on how best to characterize or describe Africa's postcolonial development challenges, there is little dispute over the fact that the attainment of political independence had not automatically resulted in sustained economic growth and the well-being of the masses of the people.[16] For scholars like Frimpong-Ansah and George Ayittey, the 'vampire/predatory state'[17] presided over by a succession of post-independence leaders

---

12 Grosh, 1994.

13 Developed in the United States in the 1950s and 1960s in the context of ideological competition between the two superpowers, the US and the USSR, modernization theory among other things, was based on the idea of linear path to development from a traditional, agrarian society to a modern industrial, mass consumption one (see Rostow, 1960).

14 Leys, 1994; see also Mamdani, 1996; Smith, 2007.

15 Giovanni Arrighi, 2002.

16 On one hand, scholars like George Ayittey (1992; 1998; 2005), Frimpong-Ansah (1991) and Callaghy (1987; 1988) have laid the blame for Africa's post-independence underdevelopment on poor leadership, misrule and administrative ineptitude by the political elites, others, like Adedeji (2002), Ake (1985; 1996), and Mkandawire (2001; 2005) have diagnosed the problem as a combination of internal and external factors, and have concluded that unless the continent extricates itself from externally imposed development strategies, the continent will continue to be a laboratory for all kinds of foreign development experiments.

17 Frimpong-Ansah,1991; see also Ayittey, 1998.

brought the continent nothing but economic misery, famine, senseless civil wars, wanton destruction, flagrant violations of human rights and brutal repression.[18] And according to Owusu,[19] while most African countries had performed relatively well economically during the first decade of independence (1960–1970), by the mid 1970s all these gains started to erode, mainly as a result of developments in the global economy culminating in the 'crisis' or 'tragedy' of the African state, referred to above.[20]

The African 'crisis' or 'tragedy,' according to Schraeder was manifested in 'the existence of bloated, corrupt, and inefficient government bureaucracies increasingly incapable of responding to the day-to-day needs of their respective populations.'[21] And while external factors played a part in creating the 'African crisis' domestic factors also contributed to the problem.[22] Owusu argues that the internal political scene which had become synonymous with military coups d'état, civil strife and ethnic violence and political instability cannot be absolved from contributing to the crisis.

In terms of the economy, the 'African crisis' was characterized by a steep decline in the quality of life for an increasing large proportion of the population in several countries and a decline in the rate of growth in all the sectors of national economies. As observed by the World Bank, 'the average annual GDP growth rate for low-income Africa declined from 2.7 percent during 1970–80 to 0.7 percent in 1982 and reached a record low of 0.2 percent in 1983.'[23] This was accompanied by a decrease in the average income per capita as well as the average capita in food production; deterioration in the foreign exchange position of the national economy; stagnation of local manufacturing industry with capacity utilization of industrial plants below economic levels and indices of industrial production reading below negative levels.[24] The result was investment levels too low even to maintain or rehabilitate existing production capacity which inhibited the full mobilization of the national human resources in the drive for survival and development.[25]

At the African inter-state level there had been a series of collective policy proposals to deal with the crisis beginning in 1980 with the OAU summit meeting of African Heads of State and Government and the launching of the Lagos Plan of Action for the Economic Development of Africa 1980–2000 and the Final Act of Lagos Plan.[26] In addition, there was the -United Nations Program of Action for African Economic Recovery 1986–1990' (UN-PAAERD) in which

18 Ayittey, 1992.
19 Owusu, 2007.
20 See Ake, 1996; also Callaghy, 1987; Bayart, 1993.
21 Schraeder, 2004: 288.
22 Owusu, 2007.
23 The World Bank, 1986.
24 Barwa, 1995.
25 Sawyerr, 1988.
26 Maloka et al., 2002; Ake, 1996.

the African leaders put in additional efforts to restore the economic status of the African countries: this culminated in the Khartoum Declaration of 1988. This Declaration recognized human development both as a means to, and an objective of, development and proposed practical measures for strengthening and further developing human capacities.[27]

For many years (perhaps until the introduction of the New Partnership for African Development in 2002), the LPA became the most elaborate and extensively discussed African development strategy in the post-colonial era.[28] Considered the most comprehensive response by African leaders to the continent's deepening economic crisis,[29] the plan minced no words in heaping much blame for the continent's poor economic record on the international exploitative economic system and the inadequacies of the exogenous development strategies being recommended by donors. It recognized the over-dependence of African economies and aimed to restructure them on the principles of self-reliance and self-sustaining development.[30] In order to achieve this, there was the need to reposition the continent in the existing international division of labor, by changing the pattern of production from primary commodities to manufactured goods, and relying more on internal sources of raw materials, spare parts, management, finance, and technology. The pursuit of national self-reliance under the LPA aimed to encourage internally-stimulated production and to discourage the reliance on imported inputs. At the same time, there was the need for African collective reliance through pooling of resources, and greater inter-African trade and cooperation to overcome Africa's vulnerability to external forces.

The LPA was very comprehensive in capturing Africa's development dilemma and offered equally comprehensive and systematic course of action. Its recommendations were generally towards a more participatory approach of development. As argued by Ake, the LPA

> takes a holistic approach in several ways: in treating agriculture and industrial development together and being methodically attentive to the effects of the one on the other, in recognizing the integral relation of the internal and external causes of African crisis, and in seeing development as a task that must involve everyone and every sector, private and public, agriculture and industry, labor, capital, and peasantry.[31]

However, the LPA and the Final Act of Lagos could not elicit the needed support from Africa's foreign development partners, especially the Bretton Woods establishment. The LPA was criticized by the World Bank for not giving enough

27 Adedeji, 2002.
28 Adedeji, 2002.
29 Adedeji, 2002; Ake, 1996.
30 Ake, 1996:23.
31 Ake, 1996: 23–4.

room to the private sector and for not conceding to public sector reform to stimulate growth.[32] The Bank proceeded to undertake its own assessment of Africa's development crisis with the view to devising what it thought were the appropriate strategies for accelerating growth. The publication of the famous Berg report on *Accelerated Development in Sub-Saharan Africa: An Agenda for Action* (1981) was regarded as the high point of the clash of ideas between Africa and its foreign patrons on their perspectives of the continent's development situation.[33] Like the LPA, the Berg Report, as it was subsequently known, also analyzed the continent's economies sector by sector, and concluded that two decades after independence Africa had made little progress towards development. But a significant point of departure between the two was that unlike the LPA, the Berg Report blamed Africa's development crisis on bad governance or what came to be known as 'government failures.' It was argued that the state-led development model pursued by many post-independence African countries had not delivered accelerated development.[34] The key argument was that the public sector was bloated and that import-substitution industrialization as well as foreign exchange control regimes in place were inimical to long-term growth. Consequently, the Report called for the rolling back of the state from the involvement in the economy activity and the need to give the private sector more room to operate as the engine of development. African countries were asked to open up their economies to more private sector participation and to replace government-led development model with market-led model. This new model had as its key pillars, the rule of the economy by market forces through trade and financial liberalization, privatization of public enterprises and removal of subsidies and any form of state intervention. The state was to confine itself to providing the enabling atmosphere for the market to flourish.[35]

These recommendations later formed the basis of the economic reform packages or the structural adjustment policies handed down to African governments by the World Bank and other donors as conditions for aid disbursement.[36] African leaders were initially hesitant to embrace these recommendations. But in the face of deepening economic crisis and in order to secure the badly needed donor support, there was little room to maneuver.[37] Thus, with few options at their disposal, many African countries during the 1980s turned to the IFIs for financial assistance. In their new-found position of strength, these institutions in turn used policy-based lending to force African governments to carry out far-reaching economic reforms. According to Stewart, in order to reverse the imbalances and restore African countries' economies to good health, the IMF and the World Bank had to impress

32 Nyong'o, 2002.

33 Browne and Cummings, 1983; see also, Owusu 2007.

34 Browne and Cummings, 1983.

35 Ake, 2006.

36 Nyong'o, 2002.

37 Adedeji, 2002.

upon African leaders the need to undertake one form of adjustment or the other.[38] In that regard, SAPs spearheaded by the BWIs appeared to be the only viable solution to halt the deteriorating socio-economic conditions being experienced in the region, in the wake of both internal and external shocks and dislocations. Consequently, the 1980s has been described as a decade of adjustment for many countries in the region as was the case elsewhere in the developing world.[39] By the end of the 1980s, 36 of the 47 countries in sub-Saharan Africa had embarked on structural adjustment programs.[40]

The measures central to most structural adjustment policies adopted by countries in the sub-Saharan Africa were: reduction/removal of direct State intervention in the productive and distributive sectors of the economy, restricting the state's responsibility as an institutional and policy framework conducive to the mobilization of private enterprise and initiative. This emphasis on the disengagement of the state from economic activity, Kim argues, was based on conventional economic theory's claim that an optimal allocation of resources can only be obtained in a competitive, free market where prices reflect relative scarcities of the resources.[41] In other words, to get 'prices right,' it was necessary to minimize the role of the intrusive African state, which was blamed for the continent's 'economic crisis.'[42] Thus, it was believed that a lesser role for the state would give freer play to both internal and external market forces and provide the appropriate engine for a resumption of economic growth and development. Consequently, the structural adjustment policies, which came to define the economic policy terrain of many African countries, were introduced and broken down into two segments as follows: the first deals with macroeconomic stabilization measures spearheaded by the IMF, and the second with structural adjustment measures directed by the World Bank. Put together in a broad framework, adjustment measures adopted by these countries included the following salient mechanisms: reduction of public expenditure, increase of domestic savings, rationalization of state owned enterprises and liberalization of the economy, export promotion and promotion of private foreign investment. These measures, it was argued by the supporters of adjustment programs, would provide a macro-economic environment congenial to the small and informal sector entrepreneurs. In its 1989 *Long Term Perspective Study on Africa*, the World Bank projected an annual growth rate in employment in the small and micro enterprises of 6 percent over the next 30 years.

In retrospect, it could be argued that the publication and subsequent implementation of the Berg Report effectively marked the onset of the application of neoliberal political economy analysis of, and solutions to, Africa's development challenges. This new developmentality, which blamed Africa's postcolonial

38 Stewart, 1995.

39 Jespersen, 1992; Stewart, 1995.

40 Bello, 1994:30.

41 Kim, 2005.

42 Kim, 2005

development crisis on internal conditions did not only represent a significant reorientation of the postcolonial state but more importantly, it also installed neoliberalism as the leading development orthodoxy in post-colonial Africa. The neoliberal 'counter-revolution' marked a significant rupture in development practice especially within the context of the postcolonial world where a stronger role for the state in the national economy had been favored.[43]

The Rise of Neoliberalism as Development Orthodoxy

To understand this neoliberal counter-revolution and how it emerged as a hegemonic ideological construct, it is important to examine its evolution from the developments within the larger global political economy. Over the years, neoliberalism has been used to describe the theory and practice of unfettered economic liberalization. The World Bank and IMF's policy prescriptions which came to represent neoliberalism in Africa advocated a tight range of economic policy instruments. They included a strong emphasis on fiscal discipline, including prioritizing the control of inflation, restricting state spending and reducing balance of payment deficits. With roots in the classical liberal political economy of scholars such as Adam Smith, neoliberalism is based on a particular set of ideological assumptions about the relationship between the individual and the state. In classical liberal theory of late eighteenth and early nineteenth century, the state's coercive power was interpreted as the primary threat to individual freedom. But as argued by Richard Peet, neoliberalism 'is an entire structure of beliefs founded on right-wing, but not conservative, ideas about individual freedom, political democracy, self-regulating markets and entrepreneurship.'[44]

Among key neo-classical economists, whose works have influenced the resurgence of neoliberal ideas are Frederick Hayek and Milton Friedman.[45] Among other things, these theorists contend (i) that the ideal society is composed of utility-maximizing individuals with perfect information who engage in free exchange in free market democracies; (ii) that free markets, which they also call competitive or capitalist markets, need democratic governance to operate most efficiently; and (iii) that the combination of a free market economy and a democratic government is not only more economically efficient but also socially desirable. They link personal individual freedom with progress and economic development, and privilege economics over politics as the primary organizing force in society. While democratic government is necessary for capitalist markets to function freely, free societies should limit the sphere of government. Hayek describes the purpose of

43 Toye,1987.

44 Peet, 2003:9.

45 Hayek, 1944; Friedman, 1962.

democracy as 'essentially a means, a utilitarian device for safeguarding internal peace and individual freedom.'[46]

In his seminal work, *The Road to Serfdom*, written towards the end of the Second World War, western society is seen as, 'above all, an individualist civilization.'[47] He contends that during the modern period of European history the general direction of social development was one of freeing the individual from the ties which had bound him to the customary or prescribed ways in the pursuit of his ordinary activities.[48] This increasing economic freedom, he contends, led not only to rapid economic growth and the development of science and technology but also to 'the undersigned and unforeseen by-product of political freedom.'[49] Hayek equates all forms of governmental planning with socialism and maintains that, through planning, government exerts a coercive power that poses the greatest single threat to individual freedom. He argues that even minimalist infringements of property rights present a step on the *Road to Serfdom*, the title of his widely-cited book.

Friedman in one of his key works, *Capitalism and Freedom* (1962), posits that competitive capitalism, 'as a system of economic freedom and a necessary condition for political freedom',[50] provides the only guarantee for a free society. As does Hayek, Friedman maintains that government regulations—whether limiting economic activities or requiring contributions to social security—deprive citizens of some 'essential part' of this freedom.[51] He defines political freedom as 'the absence of coercion of a man by his fellow men' and suggests that '[b]y removing the organization of economic activity from the control of political authority, the market eliminates this source of coercive power'.[52] For Friedman, government should restrict its role to that of 'rule-maker and umpire' of productive activities rather than that of participant. A market orientation serves not just to increase overall economic efficiency but also provides the more crucial function of limiting the scope of government action, thus reducing the chance that a majority can exercise tyranny over a minority. Put together, the ideas of Hayek and Friedman provide the intellectual foundations for the implementation of neoliberal market-led policies in the developed as well as in the developing world.

Aside from the influence of the two thinkers discussed above, the resurgence of the new liberal agenda is also attributed to key major developments within the international political economy. First, there was a crisis of the welfare state and Keynesianism in the developed Western countries, which helped propel neo-conservative political elites into power in the United States and the United

46 Hayek, 1944:70.
47 Hayek, 1944:14.
48 Hayek, 1944:15.
49 Hayek, 1944.
50 Friedman, 1962:4.
51 Friedman :9.
52 Friedman:15.

Kingdom. Thus, the ascension to power of Britain's Margaret Thatcher and America's Ronald Reagan in 1979 and 1981 respectively helped to usher in free-market economic and liberal political reforms aimed at dismantling the welfare state in both countries.

The second key event in the international political economy, which propelled the resurgence of the new liberal agenda, was the two significant oil price hikes by the Organization of Petroleum Exporting Countries (OPEC) in 1973–74 and 1978–79.[53] This had particularly deleterious effects on non-oil exporting Third World countries, resulting in balance of payment difficulties and mounting international debt. The third key factor for the rise and dominance of neoliberalism was the collapse of state socialism in the former Soviet Union and Eastern Europe by the end of the 1980s and the consequent demands for economic *perestroika* and political *glasnost*.[54]

Governing by the Market

As noted above, the publication of the Berg Report by the World Bank in 1981 resulted from what was interpreted as a crisis of development in postcolonial Africa. The publication of the report also coincided with the crisis in the wider global economy and therefore provided an important basis for the introduction of the neoliberal agenda within the African context. The Berg Report, as noted, had concluded that the African crisis was self-inflicted, resulting from the misguided policy choices and decisions by the first generation of African leaders who had overextended the role of the state and stifled the smooth operation of the market.[55] To reverse this trend and resolve the crisis, the World Bank and the IMF proposed linking all future flows of Western financial capital to the willingness of African leaders to sign and implement a set of market-based policy prescriptions.

The main policy instrument by which the findings and prescriptions of the Berg report came to be articulated across Africa during the next decades was the SAPs.[56] These programs, which initially entailed economic shock therapy of macroeconomic stabilization and, as noted in the introduction to this book, came

53 Smith et al., 2006.

54 Peet, 2007.

55 World Bank, 1981; see also Callaghy, 1987; Bayart, 1993 on the analysis of the scope and reach of the postcolonial state.

56 The SAPs promoted economic growth through a series of deregulation and privatization activities. It can be summarized in ten points, including (i) fiscal discipline; (ii) financial liberalization; (iii) tax reform—including cutting marginal taxes; (iv)unified and competitive exchange rates; (v) secure propriety rights; (vi) deregulation; (vii) trade liberalization; (viii) privatization; (ix) elimination of barriers to direct foreign investment; and (x) removal of government subvention and subsidies on health, education, and agriculture.

to be known as 'the Washington consensus,' a term first used in 1989 by a World Bank economist, John Williamson, in an attempt to 'distill which of the policy initiatives that had emanated from Washington during the years of conservative ideology that had won inclusion in the intellectual mainstream rather than being cast aside once Ronald Reagan was no longer on the public scene.'[57] A basic tenet of the Washington Consensus was that unhindered market exchanges would be the driving force of economic growth and development:

> It involved minimizing the role of government, through privatizing state-owned enterprises and eliminating government regulations and interventions in the economy. Government had a responsibility for macrostability, but that meant getting the inflation rate down, not getting the unemployment rate down.[58]

The structural adjustment policies also represented a form of policy conditionality whereby loans from the World Bank, IMF and regional development banks, aid from bilateral donors and even private finance, became effectively conditional on the agreement by the recipient government to implement often far-reaching economic policy reforms. World Bank and IMF intervention through the conditionality associated with structural adjustment was thus to formally promote economic growth, but by imposing a very particular model of development and a narrow set of economic instruments. These external interventions significantly constrained the capacity of developing countries to experiment with their own models. As Green argues, the structural adjustment reforms were based on the assumption that the global economic integration through free trade is the effective route to promote growth, and that the benefits of growth will in the long term be beneficial to both the rich and the poor.[59]

Over time, the Washington Consensus was applied as a universal blueprint for development throughout the continent. Broadly, the key policy instruments in the implementation of the SAPs were privatization of state enterprises and downsizing of the public sector, trade and financial liberalization, fiscal austerity and tight monetary policy to reduce inflation.[60] These measures, were aimed at stabilizing the domestic economy, making it attractive for private-sector led development and attractive to foreign direct investment. As a result, across board, the SAPs emphasized export-led growth, privatization and liberalization, and the efficiency of the free market.[61] In terms of specific policies, the SAPs generally required countries to devalue their currencies against the US dollar, dismantle import and export restrictions, balance their budgets and remove price

57 Wilhelmson, 2000:254.

58 Stiglitz, 2003:230.

59 Green, 1995.

60 See Mohan et al., (2000) for detailed discussion of the theory, practice and impacts of structural adjustment policies.

61 Hoogvelt, 2001.

controls and state subsidies.[62] Justifications provided for the introduction of these policies by neoliberal theorists and commentators are plenty.[63] In my view, the neoliberal development agenda in the form of structural adjustment reforms represent a new form of *developmentality* in the postcolonial world. As discussed in Chapter 1, drawing on Foucault's idea of governmentality, the introduction and implementation of these reform policies could be seen as an attempt by the West to govern Africa and the rest of the global South through the rationalities and discipline of the market.[64] This new form of control over the former colonies in the postcolonial era unlike the colonial era is led by the IMF and World Bank, who through the transmission of neoliberal ideas and practice, and especially through the use of conditionality are able to coerce developing countries to adopt neoliberal reforms.[65] The transfer of neoliberal ideas from core to periphery and the enactment of neoliberal policy initiatives at an international level have focused on open trade, freedom of investment and the removal of regulations on capital movements. These have been difficult to distinguish from the broader processes of neoliberal globalization, which have characterized international political economy in the post-war period argues, neoliberalism has become hegemonic largely through the mechanisms of globalization and that neoliberal hegemony has been reproduced and secured through discourses of globalization, open trade and market reform.[66] Indeed, as Cox points out, these discourses have been central to World Bank and IMF rhetoric.[67] Thus far, globalization has been inextricably linked with the neoliberal agenda pursued by the IFIs, the increasing power and influence of multinational corporations, the increasing mobility of capital in global markets and the time-space compression, which results from technological advancement.

The Crisis of Neoliberal Reforms and Rediscovery of Poverty

The introduction of neoliberal reforms in Africa and elsewhere in the Global South in the form of SAPs was aimed at addressing alleged structural weaknesses of their economies and to restore such economies to good health in terms of micro-economic stabilization, low inflation and high growth rate. From the middle of the 1980s however, the SAPs were severely criticized by many institutions, including International Agencies for their inability to deliver on their stated goals. UNICEF, for example, proposed a 'SAP with a human face'[68] in view of the realization that the implementation of various austerity measures had resulted in hardships for

62 Armah, 2007.
63 See Bhagwati, 2004; Wolf, 2004; Friedman, 2007; 2008.
64 Gill, 2000.
65 Taylor, 2004.
66 Gill, 2000; 2003.
67 Cox 1996; 2002.
68 Cornia, et al., 1987.

the people in those countries. A key criticism against the Washington Consensus policies represented by the SAPs was their failure to eradicate poverty in Africa and elsewhere in the developing world. In the contrary, these countries continue to accumulate more debt and were increasingly unable to provide basic social services. The debt crisis, which as noted earlier in the chapter, was the catalyst for the introduction of the SAPs, had if anything worsened despite the therapy prescribed by SAPs—Third World debt rose from $785 billion in 1982 to $1.3 trillion in 1992. The composition also changed with a larger portion owed to the IFIs than to the private sector.[69]

The opposition to the neoliberal policies and the development agenda presented by the two institutions became prominent in the late 1990s. This renewed opposition manifested in the form of the anti-globalization movement as well as in the form of the campaign for debt cancellation by a coalition of the global justice movement led by Jubilee 2000.[70] Starting from the anti-globalization 'battle of Seattle' in 1999,[71] there has been a mounting popular pressure in the West as well as scholarly criticisms against the Washington Consensus policies. Significantly, these criticisms came from much respected scholars like Bhagwati, Sachs and inside the Bretton Woods' establishment with the World Bank's own chief economist at the time, Joseph Stiglitz, leading the fray in attacking the Washington Consensus policies as insufficient in promoting long-term growth and stability in developing countries.[72]

One of the central criticisms of the SAPs was that they lacked 'country ownership' and that that they had been prepared without any consultation with representative institutions from the societies in which they were to be implemented. According to Boafo-Arthur, 'the implementation of structural adjustment was without citizen participation or input in the formulation and implementation of the various policies.'[73] Thus both governments and civil society were totally excluded from the structural adjustment process. According to Stewart and Wang, lack of country ownership and the widespread perception that the structural adjustment policies were donor-imposed is also blamed for the failure of these policies to deliver on economic development and poverty reduction in developing countries.[74]

In apparent response to the mounting criticisms the international donor community led by the BWIs introduced what Soederberg calls, 'a new development architecture' in the form of donor support for poverty reducing strategies.[75] This, among other things, includes attempts to incorporate a new poverty alleviation discourse into the World Bank's Comprehensive Development Framework (CDF),

69 Bello, 1994; Chossudovsky, 2003.

70 Peet, 2007.

71 Bhagwati, 2000; Sachs, 2005.

72 Stiglitz, 1998; see also Chang, 2001.

73 Boafo-Arthur, 1999:53.

74 Stewart and Wang, 2006; see also Botchewey et al., 1998; Collier, 2000.

75 Soederberg, 2004.

to incorporate the ideas of social development into the theory and practice of development and to emphasize greater country ownership of policies by incorporating a role for civil society through the participation of NGOs in the design and implementation of poverty reduction policies.[76] This opening up of space in the development discourse also coincides with the movement towards what Stiglitz calls, 'post-Washington consensus.'[77] As part of this new consensus, the international donor community led by the IMF and the World Bank in the mid-1990s launched an initiative to provide special debt relief from public creditors to more than 40 'Highly Indebted Poor Countries' (HIPCs).

In 1999, this initiative was further refined and widened in what has been hailed as a new approach to development co-operation and a move towards an 'inclusive neo-liberalism.'[78] As one of the conditions of this 'new' development architecture, aid recipient countries are expected to produce a Poverty Reduction Strategy Paper (PRSP), which will make clear how they will pursue the twin goals of sustainable growth and poverty reduction. The PRSP should be results-oriented, comprehensive in scope and partnership-oriented, and should involve long-term planning and must be produced in an open and participatory manner, involving civil society in the process.[79] This new emphasis on country ownership through country-wide participation and the assumptions about the positive effects of participation is hailed to represent a paradigm shift from ineffective donor-led, conditionality-driven aid regime of SAPs to a system that puts the recipient country in the driving seat.[80] Also, as part of the new aid reform agenda, the Enhanced Structural Adjustment Facility (ESAF) which had served as a medium for financing the structural adjustment programs was replaced by the Poverty Reduction and Growth Facility (PRGF). The 'new' rediscovery of poverty is also evident in a seeming convergence between the United Nations system and the BWIs, represented by the introduction of the Millennium Development Goals (MDGs) in 2000 with specific targets towards poverty reduction. Apart from this new multilateral approach, individual countries such as the United States have also rolled out new bilateral aid programs such as the Millennium Challenge Account (MCA). Introduced in 2002, the MCA aimed at increasing the US's Overseas Development Assistance by $5billion a year within five years. As of August 2012, a total of 21 African countries including Benin, Cape Verde, Ghana, Kenya, Liberia, Mali, Rwanda, Tanzania and Uganda have benefited from the MCA, having gone through a rigorous selection criteria which include the following: *ruling justly; investing in people; and economic freedom*.[81] Put together, new multilateral and bilateral aid packages such as HIPC, PRSP and MCA focusing

76 Owusu, 2006.
77 Stiglitz, 1998; 2002.
78 Graig, 2006; see also Rückert, 2006.
79 IMF, 2004 cited in Gould, 2005.
80 World Bank & IMF, 1999.
81 See http://www.mcc.gov/pages/countries.

on strict selection criteria represent a shift towards 'selectivity' in international development cooperation.

Within the African context, this global consensus towards poverty reduction is represented by the introduction of a new continental development blue-print in the form of the New Partnership for African Development (NEPAD).[82] As noted earlier, Africa's postcolonial development process had been characterized by debates between those who wanted 'homegrown' solutions for the continent's problems on one hand, and those who argued for the application of theories and ideas developed from outside. Thus, as noted above, the introduction of neoliberal policies from the early 1980s onwards represented a victory for external forces led by the BWIs who had forcefully emphasized the application of market-led neoliberal reforms in response to the so-called 'African Tragedy.'[83] But by the end of the 1990s, it became apparent that these reform policies had become discredited resulting in attempts at finding scapegoats within aid recipient countries. Thus, in order to shift the blame away from the inability of structural adjustment policies in achieving sustainable growth, the international donor community led by BWIs begun to frame aid policies around the discourses of good governance and democracy.[84] It was within this context that NEPAD was conceived by African leaders with the blessing of Western donors as Africa's response to the growing prioritization of ideas of good economic and political governance as prerequisites for development. There have been various interpretations of the emergence of NEPAD. One such interpretation is the one offered by critical scholars such as Francis Owusu and Ian Taylor.[85] According to these scholars the NEPAD initiative with its emphasis on 'partnership' between African governments and their Western donors as well as the promotion of the ideals of good governance, trade and security represents a convergence of ideas between African leaders and the West as far as postcolonial development policy is concerned. Indeed, according to Owusu,[86] NEPAD represents a shift or the death of the dependency paradigm of early postcolonial African leaders, resulting in the embrace of pragmatic neoliberalism. While there is some merit in this perspective, I would add that the NEPAD agenda with its emphasis on 'partnership,' 'good governance' and trade, needs to be understood within the context of the discursive shift which occurred towards the end of the 1990s and occasioned by a number of significant events including the Asian financial crisis, the end of the Cold War, the failure of structural adjustment policies and more recently the events of 9/11 and the global war on terror. In particular, under the NEPAD blue-print is the emphasis on a Peer Review Mechanism (PRM) by which African leaders are expected to 'voluntarily' submit themselves to their peers for performance evaluation. This, I suggest, fits perfectly

82 http://www.nepad.org.

83 Smith, 2006.

84 Abrahamsen, 2000.

85 Owusu, 2006;Taylor, 2006.

86 Owusu, 2003; 2006.

into a new cluster of mechanisms being marshaled by donors to govern countries in Africa at a distance while relying on mechanisms of self-censorship and self-policing. This governance at a distance, in my view is particularly supported by the fact that under NEPAD, adherence to a set of 'good governance indicators' is pre-requisite for continuance support from the development 'partners' such as the US, EU, G8, OECD and of course, the IFIs.

A New Development Architecture or Reinvention of Neoliberalism?

The introduction of the poverty reduction framework by the World Bank and IMF in December 1999 on paper presents a radical departure from the structure adjustment programs they had spearheaded in the Global South for more than a quarter of a century. The PRSPs framework was evolved in 1999 as part of the debt relief conditionality under the Enhanced Highly Indebted Poor Countries (HIPC2) debt relief initiative. Its essence was to ensure the proper use of resources to be released through debt relief for poor countries. The World Bank and the IMF have since designed new lending profiles to support the implementation of PRSPs-the Poverty Reduction Support Credit (PRSC), and the Poverty Reduction and Growth Facility (PRGF) respectively.

The importance of PRSP at the international level is also underscored by the fact that donor agencies are increasingly redesigning their aid portfolios and coordinating it in support of the PRSPs. Part of the commitment under the Monterrey Consensus is that donors and Western countries endorsed the *Rome Declaration on Harmonization* in February 2003, which encourages donors to harmonize their development assistance to developing countries to be centered on the implementation of the PRSPs.[87] What is new about PRSPs is that they set the fight against poverty at the heart of development policies and emphasize the importance of dialogue on development strategies. The approach and emphasis in the PRSPs is about the process through which development policies are developed, implemented, and monitored. The underlying assumption is that for policies to be meaningful and realizable the process through which they are formulated must be inclusive with popular participation in them. This new thinking about poverty reduction and development is related to the emerging dominant discourse on those issues. An emerging paradigm on development views development as freedom.[88] It means the freedom to make choices in the political, economic and social arena, and for the people to participate in making decisions that affect them or in the least for them to be consulted on those issues. But are we to take these assumptions and the official narrative for the introduction of the PRSPs on their face value? In other words, how can we interpret the new poverty reduction discourse? The

---

87 See for e.g.http://www.aidharmonization.org/ah-wh/secondary-pages/why-Rome Declaration; http://www.who.int/hdp/publications/1b_rome_declaration.pdf.

88 Sen, 1999.

emergence of the new poverty reduction discourse does not offer any departure from the core neoliberal ideas which have been promoted by the IFIs and donor countries over the years. Rather, these new policies should be seen as an attempt by these institutions to repackage their policies in response to a series of international crisis and the demands for a post-Washington consensus. As argued by Soederberg the so-called new development architecture represents an attempt by the IFIs to reinvent themselves and to respond to 'threats to neoliberalism' including the Asian Financial crisis of the late 1990s.[89] To also understand the emergence of the PRSP framework, it is important to assess these new policies within the context of the recent aid policies of the world's only remaining super-power and the bastion of neoliberal capitalism, the United States of America. In particular, it is important to critically examine the set of policies introduced and implemented by the United States government in the wake of the September 11, 2001 terrorist attacks. In particular, the introduction of the Millennium Challenge Account (MCA), I argue, represents an attempt by the US to tie its aid and development policy to the so-called War on Terror which was declared by President George Bush in the aftermath of the terrorist attacks. There are striking parallels between the US aid policy during the present post-September 11 and the post-Second World War policies of President Truman discussed earlier. Similar to the post-Second World War practice of using development aid as mechanism for securing the 'Third World' from the threat of communism,[90] the introduction of the MCA by the Bush administration as Soederberg argues, 'reflects the ongoing transformation of American imperialism, which has become more explicit after the tragic events of September 11, 2001.'[91] And as she argues, the adoption of the MCA has more to do with the so-called Bush Doctrine which is captured in both the project for the New American Century and the 2002 American National Security Strategy (NSS).[92] This linkage of security with development or what Mark Duffield calls, 'securitization of aid' has become the central component of development policy and aid cooperation between rich and poor countries.[93] With specific respect to the MCA and the criteria for qualification, the Bush administration framed 'failed states' as security risks and potential safe heavens for terrorists. On the other hand, as argued by Emma Mawdsley, a critical examination of the new policy prescriptions that accompany

89 Soederberg, 2006.

90 Escober, 1995.

91 Soederberg, 2006.

92 The 'Bush doctrine' or strategy according to George Bush (cited by Soederberg, 2006) 'will based on a distinctly American internationalism that reflects the union of values and our national interests; the aim of which will be to help make the world not just safe but better. Our goals on the path to progress are clear: political and economic, peaceful relations with other states, and respect for human dignity.'

93 Duffield, 2004.

both the PRSP and the MCA emphasize the implementation of neoliberal policies such as trade liberalization, removal of subsidies and privatization.[94]

The shift towards 'selectivity' in international aid represented by the MCA and other bilateral as well as multilateral arrangements could also be traced to the work of leading World Bank economists, Craig Burnside and David Dollar, who argued that aid only works in countries pursuing sound economic policies. The World Bank's 1998 report *Assessing Aid* concluded that a 'good policy environment' is an essential precondition for effective development assistance.[95] The report claimed that if a poor country has high trade barriers, a misaligned exchange rate, unstable prices and weak public finances, it is infertile soil for economic growth regardless of amount of aid poured into that country. It is contended that aid does work better in countries with honest governments and sound policies. Given the social challenges posed by the implementation of these policies for countries like Ghana and the unwillingness of rich countries to transform the global economy and to embrace poor countries' demand for fair trade, it is obvious that poverty reduction is not necessarily the real objective for the introduction of the new poverty reduction agenda. This agenda, in many ways, represents an attempt by the IFIs and powerful countries like the US to create the conditions for capital and as a safeguard against the proliferation of terrorist groups that might pose security threats to Western interests.

In my view, the recent rhetoric of policy change by the IFIs has not altered the power relations embedded in the politics of international development cooperation. The new poverty reduction discourse and specifically, the PRSPs framework embody this new rhetoric. As argued by Jane Parpart, participatory approaches have emerged in response to criticisms against top-down development planning and aimed at empowering aid recipient countries.[96] Parpart eloquently captures the nature of opposition to the top-down policies implemented prior to the unveiling of the new framework:

> Environmentalists warned of unsustainable growth and devastated ecologies; Feminists questioned the patriarchal nature of development discourse and practice; Post-structuralists argue that development discourse was designed to silence southern voices to control knowledge and spread Western capitalism around the globe.[97]

In apparent response to these and other criticisms, the World Bank made 'participation' the cornerstone of its 2000/2001 World Development Report (WDR). But as my case study and analysis in Chapter 3 have shown, the emphasis on participation as a means for creating space for citizens' involvement in the

94 Mawdsley, 2007.
95 World Bank, 1998.
96 Parpart, 2002.
97 Parpart, 2002: 43.

development policy making process remains a mere rhetoric. Apart from the failure of the new participatory poverty reduction framework to translate into the empowerment of the poor, participation has also been used as mechanism to selectively exclude certain groups and to co-opt others into the neoliberal agenda.

The implementation of the PRSP in Ghana, as will be illustrated in subsequent chapters, suggests a disconnect between rhetoric of participation and empowerment as propagated by the IFIs on one hand, and the visible exclusion, disempowerment and co-optation which occurs on the other hand. Thus, the new poverty reduction discourse contrary to the claim of empowerment, in fact, serves as mechanism for domination of the 'Third World.'[98] And as Cingranelli and Abouharb argue, contrary to the official narrative that the PRSP framework has created space for greater participation and empowerment of the 'Third World' in development policies and knowledge, the reality is that the PRSPs are merely a façade masking the status-quo approach to development embodied in the Structural Adjustment Policies of the IMF.[99] There are striking parallels between the post Second World War modernization/development approach towards the global South and the Cold War aid politics and the 'war on terror.' Aid is used as a disciplinary mechanism and to legitimize neo-liberal intervention. The IFIs as agents of neo-liberal capitalism have sought to re-enforce their domination over the developing world through the use of seductive language of poverty. Similarly, the US, in the post-September 11 era and in line with its new National Security Strategy (2002) has sought to reward allies and punish foes.[100] Both the PRSPs and the MCA embody the donor-imposed, conditionality laden framework of SAPs and are therefore a perpetuation of neo-liberal capitalist agenda masked in the language of pro-poor or what some analysts call, 'structure adjustment in the name of the poor.'[101]

From the foregoing, it could be surmised that the new poverty reduction discourse in many ways represents a continuity of ways in which 'development' knowledge and its propagation have been undertaken over the years through the hegemonic practices of dominant actors within the global system. The actors, ranging from Western political leaders to institutions of global economic governance by virtue of their enormous wealth and domination over institutions of global governance are responsible for development knowledge construction. The knowledge which they construct is however biased and shaped by their prejudices and from the standpoint of superiority. The non-Western world is seen as the uncivilized other of the West that is incapable of making informed decisions and therefore must be dominated. In order to understand the mechanisms by which development knowledge is constructed and how the recent poverty reduction discourse is a perpetuation of this agenda calls for a critical examination of the evolution of development theory. As will be shown by my analysis of the PRSP

98 Weber, 198.

99 Abouharb and Cingranelli, 2007.

100 Abrahamsen, 2004.

101 Mawdsley, 2007; See also Malaluan and Guttal, 2002

process in Ghana, power is manifested through the various ways in which certain ideas are reproduced, exported, and adopted. As Parpart argues, 'knowledge is not something that just exists out there, ready to be discovered and used … [it] is embedded in social contexts, exerted in relations of power and attached to different power positions.'[102] Thus, the power of the international institutions in regards to development knowledge particularly that of the IFIs, is wielded most potently through their hegemonic ability to reproduce certain ideas and garner support for them through consensus.

Consequently, I argue that the 'poverty reduction' discourse being promoted by the BWIs and the US represents a new form of social control and governing technology which are a part of a broad set of mechanisms being employed by agents of neoliberal capitalism led by the US and the two IFIs to re-enforce the dominance of the neoliberal economic agenda. These new policies, I have shown, are attempts by US as well as the IFIs to secure the expansion of the neoliberal mode and the reproduction of neoliberal hegemony through coercing developing countries in particular into implementing a neoliberal, market-led policy agenda in return for receiving funds. I have argued that far from the claim that these new poverty reducing interventions are a shift from market fundamentalist policies of structural adjustment, these instruments are deeply embedded in the principles and policies of American-led neoliberal capitalism where countries in the global South are constructed as the 'other' of the West, and as being 'highly indebted and poor' and/or 'undemocratic,' so as to justify their incorporation into the neoliberal empire. In particular, an analysis of Western development policies within the framework of post-9/11 American-led foreign policy calculations suggests a move towards the securitization of aid where development aid is stringently tied to the security agenda of the fight against terrorism.

Summary and Conclusion

This chapter sought to place the new architecture of aid as manifested in the poverty reduction strategy policies in the context of more than two decades of neoliberal reform advocated by IFIs in postcolonial regions by exploring the rise, evolution and application of neoliberal development agenda in Africa. I argue that current poverty-reduction turn in international development cooperation cannot be properly understood without an adequate understanding of the historical context that gave birth to it. I have argued that the historical aid relationships established by the structure adjustment policies of the last two decades are important in analyzing the evolution and the contents of the new poverty reduction framework. Thus the past two decades of neoliberal reform policies provide a historical context in which to analyze and evaluate the poverty reduction process in Africa. The chapter also discussed in detail what came to be known as the 'African crisis' and

102 Parpart, 2002:49.

how this provided the justification for the neoliberal intervention. It was argued that while the internal factors that gave rise to the 'crisis' were self-afflicted, the external factors were brought about by developments within the global economy. The chapter also examined the implementation of the neoliberal agenda in the form of structural adjustment programs, arguing that while the introduction of the policies were justified on overall ill-health of the various countries' economies, these policies failed not only to provide a long-term solution and to address issues of widespread poverty and social development. The chapter then traced the introduction of what is sometimes called a new architecture of aid not only to the failure of SAPs but also as response to widespread criticism from within and without the neoliberal establishment, including calls for a move towards a 'post-Washington Consensus.' While conceding that the new reform agenda in many ways could be seen as an attempt by the donor community led by the World Bank and the IMF to reinvent itself and thereby incorporate a social agenda, the chapter concludes that the best way to test the veracity of these claims made on behalf of this new agenda and to determine whether it in fact offers any departure from the previous agenda, is to examine the implementation of the new policies within specific case study. In other words, implementation of the new aid architecture requires a critical evaluation and analysis. It would be useful to assess how the micro-economic policy prescriptions in the PRSP document are different from those prescribed by SAPs. Most importantly it will be significant to examine how a country like Ghana has managed the transition from the SAPs to the PRSPs and what, if anything has changed in the nature and extent of poverty. This is the focus of the next two chapters. In Chapter 3, I draw on Ghana as a case study to analyze the implementation of the SAPs, as well as the shift from the SAPs to the new architecture of aid.

Chapter 4
Neoliberalism and the Transformation of Development Policy in Ghana

Introduction

'The idea that Africa can make a choice about whether it wants to embrace the West or not is a displaced metaphor,' Oyèrónkẹ́ Oyewùmí argues. She goes on to insist that, the more important 'point is Africa is already locked in an embrace with the West; the challenge is how to extricate ourselves and how much. It is a fundamental problem because without the necessary loosening we continue to mistake the West for self and see ourselves as the other.'[1] This chapter draws on data from my field trip in Ghana, which included interviews with public, civil society and private sector stakeholders, as well as a critical review of other primary and secondary materials in order to think through the implementation of the new poverty reduction framework in Ghana.

The chapter assesses Ghana's experiment with the new aid framework being promoted by donors within the rubric of poverty reduction strategies. For over three decades, Ghana has been at the forefront of the implementation of World Bank and IMF guided policies. The country has implemented wide-ranging reforms since the launch of the economic recovery programs in 1983. It signed the HIPC initiative in 2001 and since 2002 it adopted and began the implementation of the poverty reduction strategy. This long relationship makes Ghana an excellent case study for understanding the shift from SAPs to PRSPs within the African context.

In order to understand the shift from SAPs to the PRSPs and to identify the continuities and discontinuities between the two, it is important to provide both the genealogy of the evolution from SAPs to PRSPs and a general overview and analysis of Ghana's postcolonial political economy. The chapter will trace the evolution of the recent poverty reduction policies to the implementation of their earlier structural adjustment policies. The chapter will assess the impact of these adjustment programs on Ghana's development process as an important context for the emergence of the PRSPs. The remainder of this chapter examines Ghana's past two decades of economic restructuring under the auspices of the IMF and the World Bank. In particular, the chapter highlights the social limits of neoliberalism in Ghana as reflected in the country's inability to bridge the rural-urban poverty profile and to provide for the basic social services to the majority of its citizens. In Ghana, and across much of Sub-Saharan Africa, neoliberalism is primarily

1 Oyewùmí, 1997:25.

associated with the one-size-fits-all macroeconomic policy prescriptions. Whatever the country, these prescriptions called for deregulation, currency devaluation, trade and financial liberalization, privatization of parastatals and reduction of public enterprises. In Ghana, for example, the commitment to privatization has led to user-fees in health and education, putting both public goods out of reach of large swaths of the population.

Overview of Ghana's Postcolonial Political Economy

Ghana, under the leadership of Kwame Nkrumah became the first Sub-Saharan African country to attain political independence. In view of its favorable mineral resource base and relatively literate population, the country held a lot of promise and many had predicted that it was poised for accelerated economic development.[2] In the 1950s, Ghana was the world's leading exporter of cocoa with an annual average output of 370,000 tons.[3]

By the criterion of per capita income, Ghana was a middle-income country, judged to be the richest or at least one of the richest countries in Sub-Saharan Africa.[4] In the 1960's, Ghana's per capita income of $490 was approximately the same as that of Mexico and South Korea, although this does not mean that Ghana and these countries are similar in other respects.[5] Furthermore, Ghana was reputed to have had more stock of educated and skilled manpower than any other country in Sub-Saharan Africa.[6] At independence, the country was also endowed with rich mineral deposits like gold, diamonds and bauxite, and had an abundant supply of arable land and a relatively favorable climate necessary for agriculture expansion.[7]

On the basis of its material and human advantages, there was a general consensus among academic and development experts that Ghana would become an economic showpiece in no time.[8] To be sure, the first Republic under founding President Nkrumah saw attempts at laying foundations for accelerated economic development through socialist and centralized planning economic policies.[9] A wide range of welfare and people centered policies, including universal free education, expansion in educational and health facilities, and low cost or affordable housing scheme were introduced.[10] In terms of access to education and health care, the Nkrumah government did better than any other post-independence government.

2 Dzorgbo, 2001:1.
3 Dzorgbo, 2001:2.
4 Killick, 1978.
5 Herbst, 1993; Shaw, 1993, both cited in Dzorgbo 2001:2.
6 Shillington, 1992.
7 Kanbur, 1995.
8 Austin, 1964; Hyden, 1983: xi cited in Dzorgbo, 2001.
9 Shillington, 1992.
10 Shillington, 1992.

For instance, the number of primary schools was increased from 1083 in 1951 to over 8000 by 1966. Ghana also became the first country in the developing world to attain universal and compulsory free basic education by 1961.[11]

As suggested by Dzorgbo, the poor legacy of colonialism at holistic development meant the commitment of huge financial resources by the Nkrumah government into long-term infrastructure and human development.[12] This resulted in the construction of a number of new secondary schools, teacher training collages, post-secondary institutions such as the Cape Coast University and the Kumasi Collage of Technology (now Kwame Nkrumah University of Science and Technology) and the School of Administration at the University of Ghana.[13] In economic development, the Nkrumah government also implemented a rather ambitious expansionary industrialization program, which culminated in the opening of numerous State-Owned Enterprises (SOEs). The building of the multi-million Akosombo hydro-electric dam, the Tema Industrial Township and Motorway as well as the Industrial Development Corporation (IDC) was aimed at laying the grounds for the country's industrial take-off. These achievements are summarized by Dzorgbo as follows:

> The period of from 1951 to 1966 *(when Nkrumah became Leader of Government Business under British rule to when he was toppled)* was epochal for the breathless attempts made by Nkrumah and the CPP regime to develop Ghana and restructure socioeconomic processes through a rapid and comprehensive industrialization program in order to create a socialist society … the CPP regime took the development of Ghana very seriously. Its achievements are unparalleled so far for Ghana's postcolonial development history, and contrasts sharply with the underdevelopment of the immediate colonial past, showing the extent to which the colonial authorities had deprived Ghana of socioeconomic development.[14]

Overall, Nkrumah's aggressive socialist policies are said to have made basic services and necessities accessible to the majority of the people, and laid the foundation for long-term growth through unprecedented levels of investment in education, healthcare, electrical power and road networks. Nkrumah however operated in a hostile environment. Indeed, Nkrumah's biggest misfortune was that he was confronted by hostile forces on all fronts. At home, he faced an intolerant local political class who despised Nkrumah's rise from 'nowhere' to power.[15] Then

---

11 Shillington, 1992.

12 Dzorgbo, 2001.

13 Dzorgbo, 2001:163.

14 Dzorgbo, 2001: 184–5.

15 Nkrumah whose parents were from Nzema in the Western region of Ghana was seen as an outsider by the predominantly Ashanti local elites who had led the independence movement before inviting Nkrumah to join as a Secretary General. Nkrumah's formation of the break-away CPP from the then dominant United Gold Coast Convention (UCC) in 1949

from abroad, he was confronted by a hostile former colonizer and her Western allies who were unwilling to see a former model colony becoming the champion of socialism and state-led development model in an independent Africa, in an era of ideological warfare with the Eastern socialist bloc. Tragically for him, Nkrumah played into the hands of his opponents at home and abroad.

At home, the introduction of the Preventive Detention Act (PDA) in 1958 and the Promulgation of the One-Party Act in 1964, effectively making his ruling CPP the only legal party, mobilized the political opposition, embolden critics and alienated him from the masses.[16] On the world stage, not only did Nkrumah's increasing global stature as a spokesperson for an independent Africa and the rest of the global South alienate him from the former colonial powers, but also his incessant attacks on Western imperialism made him a prime target for those who favored regime change.

Barely six months into Ghana's independence, the American Central Intelligence issued a poignant and telling report: 'The fortunes of Ghana—the first Tropical African country to gain independence will have a huge impact on the evolution of Africa and Western interests there.'[17] Nkrumah, along with other Southern leaders had publicly professed 'non-alignment' in their dealings with the two super-powers. Yet, he left nobody in doubt as to where his heart truly lay. In order to stem the growing threat on his life and the creation of what he called a 'model socialist African country,' Nkrumah introduced a number of measures, including proscription of all political parties, except the ruling party.

The strength of Nkrumah's development plans were tested with a fall in cocoa prices in 1966. '[His] regime was deprived of critical foreign exchange and thus came to experience crisis in the management of the economy and development.'[18] Within a decade after gaining political independence Ghana's economy went into a recession, which but for brief periods of temporary relief, continued for over two decades. Output of the country declined while population increased at an even faster rate. Exports dropped both in volume and in value, as cocoa exports fell below levels achieved in the 1950s. As the foreign exchange constraint became more severe, imports contracted. Other macroeconomic indicators pointed to an evident decline in the Ghanaian economy as inflation soared higher and imbalances on both the domestic and external accounts became a permanent feature.

Amidst growing economic difficulties and accusations of intolerance for political dissent, the Nkrumah government was toppled in a military coup d'état in February 1966 while the President was away on a UN peace mission to Vietnam, setting the tone for an era of political instability and economic decay. The collapse

---

was seen as a slap in the face and there was every effort to stop him both before and after independence (see Dzorgbo, 2001;Shillington 1992; Nkrumah, 1957).

16 The PDA allowed persons considered to be threat to national security to be detained without trial. It was introduced following incessant assassination attacks on Nkrumah.

17 Cited in Quist-Adade, 2007:231.

18 Dzorgbo, 2001:312.

of the Ghanaian economy and descent into an era of political stability has been described by some as the classic failure of the postcolonial African state to live up to the promise and expectations of political independence.[19] Thus, for some scholars including the American-based Ghanaian economist, George Ayittey, postcolonial leaders such as Nkrumah with time proved unable and unequal to the challenges of governance in the post-independence era, and thus 'betrayed' the promises of the liberation struggle.[20]

While there is some merit in such arguments, any discussion on economic management and the political orientation of postcolonial leaders need to be placed within the context of not only the prevailing internal and global geopolitical environment, but also the historical legacy of colonialism and imperialism. As noted earlier, the hostile domestic political environment as well as the Cold War global environment posed many challenges for both the personal and political survival of Nkrumah. Notwithstanding all these challenges, the Nkrumah government, through its ambitious development policies laid solid foundations in education, health care, energy and transportation. Of course, Nkrumah and his government had their shortcomings, just like any modern government made up of humans and not angels. But to suggest that overall, the Nkrumah government left Ghana worse off would be contrary not only to available facts but also the monumental evidence of the physical legacies of his regime.

It is rather ironic that at the time Nkrumah was being criticized both at home and abroad for his centralized policies and 'authoritarian' tendencies, others elsewhere in the global South were embarking on similar projects, and are today reaping the benefits of pursuing their own country-tailored policies, drawing on their own indigenous political institutions.[21] The recent phenomenal growth rates in the 'Asian Tigers' and the rise of China under brutal dictatorships seem to suggest the linkage between multiparty democracy and economic development is hugely exaggerated, if not mischievous.

What is even more intriguing is the fact that the 'star pupils' of the neoliberal development agenda in Africa including Ghana and Uganda, and elsewhere including Chile and Indonesia, attained those accolades under very repressive and authoritarian regimes. Thus, while not condoning or justifying any human rights abuses on the part of the Nkrumah government, it is equally misleading to justify the overthrow of his government on the altar of economic mismanagement and authoritarianism.

Contemporary developments in the global political economy including adoption of state-interventionist policies in the face of the recent financial crisis as well as the proliferation of all kinds of regional economic and political blocs and coalitions, if anything at all, have vindicated Nkrumah's political and development strategy for independent Africa. While fiercely advocating for socialist development strategy

19 Ayittey, 1998.
20 Ayittey, 1998.
21 Mkandawire, 2001; Amsden, 1991; Evans et al., 1985.

at home, Nkrumah also became a passionate advocate for, and standard bearer of, Pan-Africanism and continental union government, believing that the unification of Africa was a prerequisite for postcolonial development and survival.[22] To be sure, Nkrumah made his Pan-Africanist ambitions very clear on the very day of Ghana's birth (March 6, 1957) by conceiving Ghana's independence in much broader terms as a prelude to the total liberation of the African continent from colonial bondage, insisting Ghana's independence would be meaningless unless it was linked with the total liberation of the African continent.[23] In order to achieve this goal, Nkrumah and his government committed much of Ghana's resources to all forms of African liberation activities, including the hosting of conferences, foreign travels across and Africa and the rest of the world and in support for African liberation movements.[24] While many Ghanaians were initially enthusiastic and supportive of this agenda, the political opposition begun to capitalize on the growing public frustration and skepticism, portraying Nkrumah and his government as insensitive to domestic problems and concerns.[25]

As the renowned scholar and Pan-African writer, Ali Mazrui, noted, it was Nkrumah's zealousness for the continental union agenda and international statesmanship, to the perceived neglect of his domestic constituency, which became his political undoing, culminating in the coup which toppled him in 1966.[26] In my view, Nkrumah's legacy, both as a Ghanaian leader and Pan-African is

22 Pan-Africanism, which had as its forebears, Edward Wilmot Blyden from West Indies and W.E.B. Du Bois, Marcus Garvey, both distinguished African-Americans, was dedicated to promoting the ideals of 'Africaness' and solidarity the struggle for African liberation. Nkruamh became involved in this movement during his days in the U.S. as a student and played a key role in the organization of the Fifth Pan-African Congress, held at Manchester England in 1944 (see http://en.wikipedia.org/wiki/Pan-Africanism). Dedicating the success of the anti-colonial struggle to the founders of Pan-African movement on the day of Ghana's independence Nkrumah said, 'Marcus Garvey looked through the world if he could find a government of a Black people. Marcus Garvey did not find one. And he said he was going to create one. Marcus Garvey did not succeed. But today, the dreams of Garvey … and all those who have gone before us come to reality at this present moment' (cited by Quist-Adade, 2007:224); also see Nkrumah, 1957; 1963.

23 Nkrumah, 1957:x.

24 In 1958, Nkrumah hosted the first All African Peoples' Congress and in the year, Ghana gave huge financial support to Guinea to survive their independence after the colonial power had vowed to deny them any form of support for voting against the proposals for a 'French Community' comprising France and her colonies. Ghana also became home and a source of inspiration for a countless number of African liberation leaders and future Presidents, including Julius Nyerere, (Tanzania) Kamuzu Banda (Malawi) and Robert Mugube (Zimbabwe). He was the chief architect behind the formation of the Organization of African Unity in 1963, even though his demand for immediate continental union government was voted down (see Nkrumah, 1963).

25 Frimpong-Ansah, 1991:76.

26 Based on this Mazrui (2002) concludes that Nkrumah was 'a great African but not a great Ghanaian.'

unrivalled. The transformation of the Organization African Unity to the African Union with structures identical to some of Nkrumah's original ideas, in my view, is an enduring testimony to Nkrumah's vision and astuteness. While in the 1960s few shared his vision of African unity based on common currency, central bank, military high command and common immigration policy, today all these ideas have been appropriated and adopted by the Europeans and Africans alike. Nkrumah's blueprint for Africa's political survival, economic development and internal security are the very ideas being pushed not only by Africans in the form of the African Union and the NEPAD, but also by today's disciples of globalization and integration. These recent developments and the growing interest in Nkrumah's vision have led Mazrui to conclude:

> Although leaders like Qaddafy, Julius K. Nyerere and Nelson Mandela have been important in the annals of African unification, Kwame Nkrumah remains the biggest name in the politics of Pan-Africanism in the last one hundred years. No other single individual in this period of history has been more symbolic of the Pan-African dream than Nkrumah. His Pan-African symbolism has continued and will persist long after his death in Romania in 1971.[27]

The Political Economy in the Post-Nkrumah Era

Ghana's political economy in the post-Nkrumah era was an abysmal failure. In the political front, a series of military coup d'états, counter coups interspersed by stints of civilian rule created an atmosphere of political instability. As to be expected, the impact of the political situation on the economy was monumental. Across the board, all indicators by the end of the 1970s showed an economy in a free fall if not virtually collapsed: annual inflation, which was below 10 percent in 1970 rose to 40 percent in 1975 and exceeded 100 percent in 1983. Government revenue dropped from over 16 percent of GDP in 1975 to just 7 percent in 1983. Public sector investment plunged from around 6 percent of GDP in the mid 1970s to less than 1 percent in 1983, resulting in a severe deterioration in the nation's economic and social infrastructure. Between 1975 and 1983 real GDP fell dramatically and real income per capita fell by 27 percent. Thus, by the early 1980s the Ghanaian economy was in a very critical condition. The effect of the economic decline on social services was especially deleterious. Real per capita expenditure on health fell from 6.4 percent of total expenditure in 1974 to 0.6 percent in 1983/1984. By 1984, half of medical practitioners had left the country. And with shortages of drugs, materials and personnel, hospital attendance dropped substantially. Food supplies became limited: per capita food availability in 1983 was 3 percent lower

27 Mazrui, 2001.

than in 1974. The food price indices for locally produced food in 1970, 1980 and 1983 were 11,393 and 2,755 respectively.[28]

From the foregoing, it is clear that the overthrow of Nkrumah and the experimentation with different forms of national economic management did little to tame the tide of economic decline. By 1983, the country's economy was a classic example of stagflation: inflation was running at 123 percent and output was declining at an average of about 1 percent per annum. There was shortage of almost every conceivable item: food, raw materials and even water. Ghana's economic crisis could be described in the following terms: first, failure of the development strategies pursued since independence, which focused on large-scale state-owned enterprises dependent on imported raw materials and heavily protected by the state; second, falling savings and investment in the private and public sectors along with falling output and accelerating inflation; and third, external shocks—severe droughts of the early 1980s, expulsion of nearly one million Ghanaians from Nigeria in 1983 and plummeting cocoa prices.[29]

Against this background, the Government failed to provide adequate incentives for producers in the primary product sector which generated the bulk of the country's foreign exchange via exports.[30] It was compounded by the failure to apply normal commercial and financial disciplines to the large number of new industries set up in the public sector which is believed to have contributed to corruption and embezzlement.[31] As a result, the growth of output had come to a halt and then turned negative beginning from 1975 until 1982, while real per capita income declined by more than 30 percent and the overall balance of payments deficit widened leading to a depletion of foreign exchange reserves and an accumulation of external payments of deficits of about US$580 million by the end of 1982.[32] It is apparent that the causes of the decline in Ghana's economy could be attributed to structural weaknesses, external shocks—particularly, declines in the terms of trade, economic mismanagement, and political instability.

The immediate consequence of the economic decline in Ghana was the general impoverishment of the nation as a whole. Most indicators point to a drop in the standard of living in the country. Per capita GDP, at constant 1975 prices, dropped from a level of C634 in 1971 to C394.8 in 1983. Most people could not afford the basic necessities of life such as food and shelter. The index of food production per capita with 1971 as base of 100 dropped to about 72 in 1982.[33] Although available data on life expectancy showed an increase from 46 years in 1970 to about 55 years in 1979, it later dropped to 53 years at the beginning of 1980s. Other indicators point to a severe deterioration in health standards.

28 Aryeetey et al., 2000; Barwa, 1995; Boafo-Arther, 1999; Hutchful, 2002.
29 Barwa, 1995.
30 Ake, 1996.
31 Pickett and Singer, 1990.
32 IMF, 1991.
33 Dzorgbo, 2001; Hutchful, 2002.

Daily calorie supply as a percentage of minimum requirement dropped from 88 percent in 1979 to 68 percent in 1983.[34] This may have been due to the famine, which came about in 1981/82 because of the draught that hit the Sahel region. The poor economic situation also led to shortages of drugs and other supplies, which affected provision of health services. The situation was made worse by a massive brain drain, which affected the medical profession. In the education sector, data on enrolment showed an improvement over the years but it was no secret that the quality of education had fallen. As with health, the poor economic condition affected educational supplies and books, and was also made worse by the emigration of qualified teachers, particularly to Nigeria.

Another significant consequence of the economic crisis of the seventies and eighties was its effect on manpower development and labor. The high rates of inflation were not matched by the increase in the nominal wage. Thus, over the years workers saw their real income being eroded. This affected mainly those on wage incomes, and caused most of them to take on second and third jobs. The most common second job was trading. At the height of the economic crisis period, those who benefited most were traders. The 'trading' need not be in actual wares. Some people made huge gains just by knowing someone in a position to give them chits[35] for obtaining 'essential commodities'; these chits were then sold to the actual traders for cash. Such dishonest acts did not encourage manpower development in the country. School dropouts who turned themselves into 'businessmen' became better off than their counterparts who went on with their schooling. Skilled personnel like doctors, engineers and teachers who could not engage in any illegal trade, took flight from the country and even the continent. These specialized workers left mainly for other African countries and Asia. Nigeria was the main beneficiary of the Ghanaian brain drain, although most of the medical doctors ended up in Saudi Arabia. It is estimated that there were more Ghanaian doctors in Saudi Arabia than in Accra.[36] Most teachers immigrated to Nigeria since the oil boom in that country at that time had led to the establishment of new schools. By the beginning of the 1980s Ghanaians of every class and skill were leaving en masse for Nigeria. This was what led to the expulsion of almost a million Ghanaian refugees from that country in 1983, when the decline in oil revenue forced a decline in the growth of the Nigerian economy.

The Era of Structural Adjustment: The Miracle and the Mirage

In 1983, the Provisional National Defense Council (PNDC) military government of Flt. Lt. Jerry Rawlings introduced an Economic Recovery Program under

34 Hutchful, 2002.

35 One of the methods of rationing scarce commodities was through the issuance of notes of rights to purchase.

36 Oquaye, 1980.

the auspices of the World Bank and the IMF. The introduction of these reform policies marked a significant policy shift from the state-led policy framework that had been laid at the attainment of independence. The reasons for this shift could be understood within the context of the wider crisis in the postcolonial African political economy. As discussed in Chapter 2, due to a combination of internal and external factors much of the African continent had descended into a 'crisis,' which by the virtue of the World Bank's Berg Report could only be overcome through the implementation of specific market-led reforms.

The Ghanaian political scientist, Kwame Boafo-Arther, appropriately sums up Ghana's deteriorating socio-economic situation at the time: 'by the early 1980s, Ghana had reached abysmal levels in its socio-economic development. Only effective and sustainable measures could salvage the economy.'[37] It was against the backdrop of these dire economic indicators coupled with a severe draught and the expulsion of about two million Ghanaians from neighboring Nigeria that year that the Economic Recovery Program (ERP) was launched in 1983. The Recovery Program, which was Ghana's version of the structural adjustment programs already introduced in a number of African countries, culminated in the implementation of rigorous and comprehensive market-led reform policies geared towards the resuscitation of the economy.

The reform policies were in two major phases, each addressing a particular ailment identified in the economy. Phase one of the recovery program, which was dubbed the stabilization phase, lasted between 1983 and 1986. This aspect of the recovery was aimed at halting the economic decline, especially in the industrial and export commodity production sector. It involved macroeconomic stabilization measures comprising fiscal, monetary and exchange rate policies; liberalization of prices; and restructuring of the public and financial sectors. The second phase of between 1987 and 1989 was the structural adjustment and development phase and it focused mainly on growth and development with a special emphasis on the social services.[38] The key elements of the strategy for implementing the ERP have been: (a) a realignment of relative prices to encourage productive activities and exports through strengthening of economic incentives; (b) a progressive shift away from direct controls and intervention towards greater reliance on market forces; (c) the early restoration of monetary and fiscal discipline; (d) the rehabilitation of social and economic infrastructure; and (e) the undertaking of structural and institutional reforms to enhance the efficiency of the economy and encourage the expansion of private savings and investment.[39]

The implementation of SAPs resulted in a major turnaround in Ghana's overall financial and economic performance at least during the early years. During the first decade after the start of the reform policies, growth in real GDP recovered, allowing gains in per capita incomes; inflation declined and the general position

37 Boafo-Arthur, 1999:46–7.

38 Boafo-Arther, 1999.

39 IMF, 1991.

regarding balance of payments switched from deficits to surpluses, facilitating external payments and a build-up of exchange reserves. The recovery in output growth, combined with the gradual liberalization of exchange restrictions boosted the expansion in the volume of imports to an average of 10 percent a year. The rising external financing requirements have been covered in part by modestly growing inflows of private capital, including direct investment and by increase in the inflows of official external assistance. The inflows of official grants and concessional loans rose from the equivalent of less than 1 percent of GDP in 1983 to about 10 percent of GDP by 1990.[40]

During the ensuing decade, the country earned much praise from the two financial institutions as well as Western donors for being 'a good reformer and great economic performer".[41] The World Bank, in its *Adjustment in Africa*[42] report, argued that the structural adjustment policies made huge impacts at bringing countries like Ghana from near economic collapse to a semblance of stability and modest growth.[43] In terms of micro-economic stability, the recovery efforts have proved to be successful in terms of short-term growth. In 1986 GDP in real terms increased by 5.3 percent; per capita real income grew by 2.6 percent; agriculture output increased by 4.6 percent, while services expanded by 5.4 percent.[44] The country's infrastructure, which was almost non-existent at the onset of the adjustment program in 1983, also witnessed an appreciable level of repair and development. In the view of Donald Rothschild, the implementation of the SAPs in Ghana 'reversed the decline of recent years.'[45] For his part, Gibbon rated Ghana as being among Africa's most successful, pointing to the appreciable macroeconomic outrun as a result of the implementation of SAPs.[46]

By the end of the 1990s, the real impacts of the adjustment policies had begun to unfold. Despite the improvements on the economic and financial scenes, the country continued to be confronted with a number of structural, institutional and financial constraints. These included a high inflation rate; a small though developing private sector; low levels of domestic savings and investment which prevent a self-sustained growth in output; and increasing pressure on the public sector's management and implementation capacity.[47]

Also, the gains in macroeconomic stability have not translated into improved living conditions for majority of the Ghanaian population.[48] In the mid-1990s

40 For a detailed overview and analysis of Ghana's economic recovery program see Hutchful, 2002.

41 (Stamata 2001).

42 World Bank, 1994.

43 World Bank, 1993.

44 Government of Ghana, 1987.

45 Rothschild, 1991:10–11.

46 Gibbon, 1992.

47 see Dzorgbo 2001; Hutchful 2002.

48 Sachs 2005; Appiah, Demery and Laryea-Adjei 2000; Hutchful, 2002.

Ghana was ranked 133 on the HDI; in 2006 Ghana dropped to 136 after a marginal rise between 2002 and 2004. Almost half of Ghana's population lives in absolute poverty. The Ghana Statistical Service estimated that one third of the country's population continue to live below the poverty line of less than one dollar a day by 1998.[49] There was also a growing evidence of deepening poverty among certain groups and regions: five out of the country's ten regions had more than 43 percent of their populations living in poverty in 1999; six regions witnessed an increase in poverty and are now living in extreme poverty; one third of the national population cannot meet basic nutritional needs.[50] In terms of groups, food-crop farmers experienced the highest incidence of poverty: approximately 60 percent fell below the poverty line in 1998/1999.[51]

The implication of this is that, since women are pre-dominant in this category, poverty in Ghana affects women most. These figures were confirmed by the Fourth Ghana Living Standards Survey (GLSS), conducted in 1998. The study shows that the modest economic growth, which occurred under the Economic Recovery Program, had not generated the expected improvements in income required to improve consumption, and in particular to compensate for reductions in government services and subsidies. The study also showed a growing inequality and poverty among certain categories of people and in some parts of the country.

A striking feature of Ghana's poverty profile is the fact that rural poverty has been on the increase or has not seen any appreciable reduction during 'adjustment years.' The GLSS indicated that poverty in Ghana remains a rural problem, with about 80 percent of the poor living in rural areas.[52] In terms of localities, significant poverty reduction has been reported in Accra and rural forest areas, while modest reductions were recorded in other urban areas in coastal districts. Another disturbing trend in the country's economy development process, particularly after years of donor guided economic restructuring was the lack of a robust manufacturing sector resulting from the failure to diversify the country's export base.

There have been a number of studies which have compared Ghana's post-independence development with countries in East Asia.[53] These studies have shown among other things that while at time of their independence, Ghana and other African countries were at par if not ahead of their Asian counterparts on a series development indicators, by the end of the 1970s, the Asian countries had outpaced and outperformed African countries.

As pointed out by Ravi Kanbur, himself a former World Bank economist and Ghana Country Director in 1957 when Ghana and Malaysia both attained their

49 Ghana Statistical Service (GSS), 1999.

50 GSS, 1999.

51 GSS, 1999.

52 GSS, 1999.

53 Asare and Wong, 2004; Tsikata, 2007.

independence, 'Ghana's per capita GDP was several times that of Malaysia.'[54] Among the reasons cited for this disparity in development fortunes between African countries and their Asian peers, according to Kanbur, are the structural features such as constraints of 'world markets and Africa's specialization in primary commodities.'[55] According to Asare and Wong, at the time of their independence in 1957, Malaysia and Ghana started off as primary goods producers with few products.[56] For instance, in 1958, Malaysia's main export items were rubber, contributing almost 60 percent to the total export value, and tin, contributing about 12 percent.

The main Ghanaian economic activity was in cocoa production, contributing about 66 percent to the total export value. It was followed by wood (12 percent of export value), with diamonds and manganese each contributing 9 percent to the total export value.[57] However, after independence, the Malaysian government made a strong effort to diversify not only the agricultural sector but it branched out and made great inroads into manufacturing. Rubber's dominance at independence has been reduced to about one percent of Malaysia's total export value. The main agricultural export item now is palm oil, which contributes about five percent to its export value. Furthermore, Malaysia has reduced its dependence on agricultural exports to obtain foreign earnings. Manufacturing products seem to have overtaken agricultural products as the main foreign exchange earner. For example, Malaysia has become one of the largest producers of semiconductor devices in the world.[58]

The Nkrumah government had begun to diversify the economy through the establishment of a number of medium scale industries. After the overthrow of the government in 1966, these policies were either reversed or abandoned. Ghana has made little progress in economic diversification, and there is still heavy dependence on one agricultural commodity (cocoa). Cocoa exports contribute about 35 percent to Ghana's export value. The problem of dependence on one commodity, especially agricultural, as the main export is well-known. Fluctuations in the world price of that commodity can adversely affect the economy of the country and its development efforts. Moreover, weather and crop diseases can also play havoc in the production of an agricultural commodity such as cocoa. For sustained economic development, it is necessary to have multiple sources of export revenue so that a temporary disruption in one product or service does not jeopardize the funding of the country's development efforts. Manufacturing, a more efficient vehicle for rapid and sustained economic progress, has yet to attain a large scale in Ghana. As of 1999, the agricultural sector generated about 36 percent of Ghana's GDP, with the industrial and service sectors generating

54 Kanbur, 2000:410.

55 Kanbur, 2000.

56 Asare and Wong, 2004.

57 Kanbur, 2000:410.

58 Creffield, 1990:51 cited by Asare and Wong, 2004.

25 percent and 39 percent, respectively. In Malaysia, the percentages were 14 percent for agriculture, 44 percent for industry, and 43 percent for services.[59]

In the meantime, a Multi-Country Participatory Assessment of Structural Adjustment jointly carried out by the World Bank/Civil Society/Government/Structural Adjustment participatory Review Initiative (SAPRI) and the Citizens' Assessment of Structural Adjustment (CASA), was published in 2002.[60] The study brings to the fore the impacts of structural adjustment on the poor from different dimensions/perspectives, including access to social services, such as education and health and the provision of essential goods, which suffered as a result of withdrawal of subsidies. With a specific reference to Ghana, the report cites worsening levels of health and educational standards of the majority as a result of full cost recovery measures introduced in the wake of structural adjustment. It also cites the deleterious effect of privatization policies on the poor.

Another key revelation in this study is the effect of the boom in Ghana's mining industry in the wake of adjustment.[61] The study shows that aside from the often-cited environmental problems associated with excessive mining activities; there are other socio-economic dynamics to the shift of emphasis to the mining sector. These include the high cost of living within the main mining communities, resulting in the rise in prices of basic commodities beyond the reach of the average household. What is interesting is the fact that the salaries of the regular mining staff are indexed to the US dollar and this, in turn, tends to drive up prices. Also the boom in the mining industry was found to push a significant percentage of the labor force out of agriculture and other income generating activities by eliminating farmland. The consequences of this on food production and food prices are not far-fetched. And according to the study, the harsh economic conditions faced by many households as a result of the combination of these mining industry boom-related factors have pushed school-going children into menial jobs at the expense of their education.

Another study sponsored by the International Labor Organization on the impact of the implementation of the adjustment programs on Ghana's informal sector, found out that the introduction of 'user fees' for education and health services and retrenchment have resulted in a net decrease in household real incomes and an increase in the number of poor households, which by virtue of their low purchasing capacity decreased the demand for urban informal sector products. Apart from job lay-offs suffered by the people, it is also shown that as a result of subjecting privatized utilities rates to market forces, they become very inaccessible to many, particularly the poor. Again, Hutchful notes that several years of adjustment in Ghana have not resulted in any appreciable improvements in the nutrition needs, particularly of women and children. This view is supported by other studies.[62]

59 World Bank, *WDR*, 2000/2001:296 cited by Asare and Wong, 2004.

60 SAPRIN, 2004.

61 SAPRIN, 2004.

62 Hutchful, 2002.

From the foregoing, it is apparent that the implementation of the World Bank and IMF guided structural adjustment reform policies could not be said to have yielded the desired results sufficient to impact positively on poverty reduction and long-term development. While the economic recovery programs have a positive impact on the macroeconomic position, they failed to invigorate the productive sectors of the economy.[63]

The Structural Adjustment Program in Ghana has focused more on macroeconomic stabilization than on growth and poverty reduction. As Jeffrey Sachs sums up the country's current economic condition, very little headway has been made with the implementation of the World Bank and IMF-guided policies:

> Ghana suffers from considerable extreme poverty. Like other African countries, Ghana has been unable to diversify its export base beyond a narrow range of primary commodities, mainly cocoa beans. It lacks the domestic resources needed to finance critical investments in health, education, roads, power and other infrastructure.[64]

The Ghanaian economy slipped back into crisis in the third quarter of 1999. Poor macroeconomic management, particularly through fiscal indiscipline, and adverse external economic conditions—low cocoa and gold prices, and high oil prices—caused the macroeconomic fundamentals to be weak. Inflation accelerated and interest rates became unbearably high. Large fiscal imbalances persisted causing the Government to borrow more from the domestic economy, thus crowding out the private sector. The fiscal excesses have led to the rapid buildup of domestic debt. By the beginning of 2000, Ghana's domestic debt had swollen to almost 20 percent of national output, with interest payments more than the national expenditure on health and education combined. The total Government bonded domestic debt at the beginning of 2000 stood at about 9.1 trillion cedis.[65] This excluded payment arrears owed to contractors, debt of some parastatal agencies such as Tema Oil Refinery (TOR) and Ghana National Petroleum Corporation (GNPC), and also debt of subvented organizations as well as local government units. Interest payment on the debt alone was more than a third of the national recurrent expenditure and certainly more than the development expenditure.[66]

In addition Ghana had the statutory obligation of servicing its external debt. The current account-induced balance of payment difficulties of 1999 intensified into the 2000 general election year, leaving the country's foreign exchange market badly distorted.[67] The local currency (the cedi) underwent huge depreciations

63 Alderman, 1991; Desai, 1992; UNICEF 1987; Ghana/UNICEF, 1990; see Rothchild, 1991; Herbst, 1993; Tsikata, 2001.

64 Sachs 2005:272.

65 Osei and Quartey, 2001.

66 Osei and Quartey, 2001.

67 Osei and Quartey, 2001.

with variable impact on different economic groups. The impact was most severe on firms producing for domestic markets and those engaged in pure commerce. Export-oriented firms, on the other hand, perhaps on account of their foreign exchange retention entitlements and privileges, seemed to have fared better. In the final analysis, the inflationary situation in the country got worse.

Against this background, the new Kufuor-led government which assumed office in January 2001 had no option but to sign up for the HIPC initiative. This program seeks to bring the debt position of poor countries that have performed well to a level that is affordable. The IDA and IMF made a preliminary assessment of the country's eligibility in May 2001 and agreed to support Ghana under the Enhanced HIPC Initiative through the Decision point.

Genealogy of the Poverty Reduction Framework in Ghana

Like Uganda, Ghana had tried to articulate a national poverty reduction strategy, albeit with limited success long before the idea was embraced by the World Bank and the IMF as a central theme of their aid policies in September 1999.[68] The 1995 Consultative Group (CG) meeting on Ghana held in Paris marked a turning point in the government's strategy to combat poverty by establishing the institutional framework for coordinating poverty reduction initiatives countrywide. This was against the backdrop of the failure of stabilizing and adjustment policies of the previous decade to translate into changes in the productive sectors of the economy, a situation which resulted in worsening levels of poverty. The highest policy making organ on all issues relating to poverty reduction was the Inter-Ministerial Committee on Poverty Reduction (IMCPR) established in 1995 and chaired by the Minister of Finance.

The IMCPR comprised all Ministers responsible for the social sector, including health, education, employment and social welfare, agriculture, infrastructure, local government and rural development. The Heads of the National Development Planning Commission (NDPC) and the National Council for Women and Development were also members of the IMCPR. When Ghana decided to prepare a PRSP, the IMCPR was given the oversight responsibility. The IMCPR was served by an inter-agency and multi-sectoral Technical Committee on Poverty (TCOP) which provided the IMCPR with the requisite technical backstopping for ensuring effective coordination of poverty reduction oriented activities. The Poverty Reduction Unit (PRU) located at the NDPC is the Secretariat. The Director-General of NDPC chaired the TCOP. The TCOP employs the Working Group concept in promoting coordination and harmonization of ideas on poverty reduction. At the district and sector levels, the District Planning Coordinating Units (DPCUs) of the District Assemblies (DAs) and Policy, Planning, Monitoring and Evaluation Divisions (DPPMEDs) of Ministries,

68 Tsikata, 2006.

Departments and Agencies (MDAs) had the responsibility for coordinating poverty activities and technically mainstreaming poverty reduction into policies and plans.[69]

Another notable effort at poverty reduction by the Ghanaian government in the 1990s and prior to the unveiling of the PRSP framework by the Bretton Woods institutions was the preparation of the National Development Policy Framework (1994) which was later renamed Vision 2020. It proposed to turn Ghana into a middle-income country by the year 2020. It was accompanied by a five-year policy statement entitled, 'Vision 2020: the First Step', which was used as the basis for developing the First Medium Term Development Plan 1996–2000 (MTDP).[70] While these policy measures were laudable, and showed the willingness of the government to address the challenges posed by poverty, these documents were allowed to collect dust in the shelf largely as result of lack of support from donors.[71]

In its continuing effort to tackle poverty, the Government of Ghana embarked on preparing a national poverty reduction strategy paper immediately after the establishment of the Enhanced HIPC initiative in 1999 by the BWIs. The Enhanced HIPC initiative stipulated that developing countries seeking debt relief or concessional assistance from the multilateral institutions must prepare a national PRSP in consultations with their populations. This requirement also applied to countries wishing to access resources from bilateral donors. In June 2000, the outgoing government of Jerry Rawlings hastily prepared an Interim Poverty Reduction Strategy Paper (I-PRSP) in a most unparticipatory manner contrary to the guidelines. Although the government claimed at the time that the I-PRSP is based on the long-term vision contained in the Ghana Vision 2020 document, there is little evidence to confirm this claim. To the contrary, the I-PRSP was drawn from the World Bank's 2000–2003 country Assistance Strategy document. In this respect, the I-PRSP had nothing to do with poverty; and it was all about securing additional donor resources given the precarious state of Ghana's economy resulting from collapse in the country's terms of trade and escalating oil prices. It was not surprising that the joint Boards of the IMF and the World Bank approved the I-PRSP in August 2000 considering the document's intellectual roots. In return, Ghana was granted an IMF loan—Poverty Reduction and Growth Facility (PRGF), formerly known as the Enhanced Structural Adjustment Facility (ESAF).[72]

The PRGF, which would have been active until 2002, was subsequently suspended with the coming into office of the New Patriotic Party (NPP) government in January 2001. The previous government had fallen from the good graces of the IMF for failing to implement a number of prior action conditions. This had a ripple effect on the already poor state of Ghana's economy. The fragility of the Ghanaian economy despite 20 years of adjustment was evident in the financial bankruptcy

69 Government of Ghana, 2000.

70 Government of Ghana, 1998.

71 Tsikata, 2006.

72 Killick and Abugre, 2001.

of the state, which the new government of John Kufuor had to grapple with on assuming power in January 2001. The NPP government had little time to celebrate its historic electoral victory as it soon found itself in the midst of an economic crisis. The negative terms of trade, which began in 1999 as a result of the collapse of the cocoa market and the simultaneous escalation of the price of oil, deteriorated further as the national currency—the Cedi—lost half of its value in 2000 and the inflation rate reached the 40 percent range for the first half of 2001, and domestic debt interest payments were consuming half of all revenue. Faced with a huge fiscal deficit and high inflation, the new government quickly put in place a strong program of stabilization that helped arrest the economic slide. The inflation rate declined to 21.3 percent at the end of the year, and the Cedi depreciated by only 4.1 percent over 2001.

The government's willingness to implement a number of prior action conditions opened the door for the reactivation of the PRGF and the disbursement of the outstanding tranche. In addition, Ghana qualified for debt relief under the Enhanced HIPC initiative, reversing the previous government's position not to apply for HIPC status. What then are the policy implications and impacts of the new architecture of aid in Ghana? The next segment of this chapter critically evaluates Ghana's poverty reduction strategy in relation to some of the key assumptions of the new poverty reduction framework. In particular, my analysis of Ghana's poverty reduction process seeks to answer key questions raised by the shift from structural adjustment approach to poverty reduction strategies as the mechanism for international aid relationships. I explore two broad areas: country ownership; and policy choices. I draw on the concept of policy space for my discussion of these issues. I first provide a working definition of policy space before discussing in detail the role of donors and governmental actors, as well as the specific policies and how these differ from those implemented under structural adjustment.

In the Driver's Seat? The Politics of Policy Ownership

The new poverty reduction framework of the IFIs have emphasized national ownership and policy space as means for achieving economic development. The main assumption contained in this particular aspect of the recent policy shift is the belief that local ownership of policies would result in reconfiguration of the development policy-making space to include non-state actors. For over two decades, the IFIs have used their neoliberal policy prescriptions including trade and financial liberalization and privatization to constrain developing countries' autonomy and ability to design national policies. The objective of this segment of the chapter is to interrogate whether the policy prescriptions of the 'new' aid architecture help or hinder the ability of developing and aid dependent countries like Ghana to design and implement policies aimed at poverty reduction and development.

While the concept of policy space is rarely new, its usage in the context of international development is most often used in debates about how certain rules in the global economy—particularly those emanating from the WTO and its subsidiary agreements—constrain countries' policy options for medium- and long-term economic development.[73] For example, Birdsall, Rodrik, and Subramanian talk about the need for poor countries to have 'enough space to craft their own economic policy' and 'adequate room for policy autonomy and experimentation.'[74] For his part, Robert Wade describes 'development space,' as the freedom of developing countries to pursue, among other things, the kinds of development policies used in the past by what today are the world's advanced economies.[75] The United Nations Trade and Development Program (UNCTAD), has been at the forefront in highlighting the continuing shrinking of developing country policy space due to aid conditionalities. It conceptualized policy space as a fusion of the principle of sovereign equality among sovereign states, the right to development, and the principle of special treatment for developing countries.[76] In its '2004 São Paulo Consensus' UNCTAD concluded that, in the face of increased convergence between the agendas of the IFIs and the multi-lateral trading system, opportunities for national governments to determine their own policies are being reduced.

Ghana's policy making terrain prior to the emergence of the PRSP framework in the late 1990s had been largely shaped by the multilateral and bilateral aid regime overseen by the international financial institutions.[77] In that sense, there was limited autonomy for state-actors in the design and implementation of national development policies. The introduction of the structural adjustment policies from the early 1980s in the form of the Economic Recovery Program as discussed earlier marked the end of the statist development agenda and the beginning of the market-led approach promoted by the World Bank and the IMF. This resulted in the implementation of wide-ranging policy prescriptions, described as the 'Washington Consensus.' The primary vehicle that international financial institutions used to push through these market-led prescriptions, resulting in major squeeze in borrowing governments' policy space is the 'conditionalities' attached to IFI Structural Adjustment Loans (SALs) and projects. SALs are an early name for policy-based loans that IFIs have used to impose conditionalities on developing and transition countries. Besides financing policy-based loans that significantly restricted policy space, the World Bank and other Multilateral Development Banks (MDBs) also used project loans to impose conditionalities on economic policies. Agricultural, rural development, water supply, sanitation, education, health and virtually every type of conventional IFI project imposes conditionalities such as requiring developing countries to privatize services and

73 Martinez-Diaz, 2006.

74 Birdsall et al., 2005.

75 Wade, 2005.

76 South Centre, 2006:3; see also UNCTAD, 2004.

77 Whitfield, 2005.

drop tariffs unilaterally without developed country reciprocity. Thus as suggested by Ravi Kanbur, the loss of policy space within the context of structure adjustment centered around the issue of national and policy sovereignty.[78]

It was against this backdrop of the constraints imposed by the structural adjustment conditionalities that the introduction of the new poverty reduction framework must be examined in order to determine if indeed there has been a significant change in terms of the make-up of the policies as well as the terrain in which they are crafted. Indeed, as argued by Tan, whether or not the new poverty reduction framework represents a change should be determined by the extent to which, there is a shift from 'the disciplinary framework' of SAPs to 'a more inclusive framework to development policy-making.'[79] On paper, the poverty reduction framework sought to address the shortcomings of SAPs by emphasizing 'country ownership' which would ensure that policies are tailored to country specific circumstances and are generated by the country itself in a process involving a broad-base of societal and political actors. According to the Bank and the Fund, the new policy framework was aimed at ensuring 'broad participation of civil society, other stakeholder groups, and elected institutions.' This, they claim will also 'involve consultations with representatives of the poor' in order to incorporate the concerns of the broad spectrum of society into the design and implementation of development policies.[80] By emphasizing country ownership and local participation, the poverty reduction framework, at least on paper, represents move towards a post-Washington Consensus framework or a move towards what some have called 'inclusive neoliberalism.'[81] While the claims made by BWIs in regard to the new poverty reduction framework are laudable, the only way to determine or test the applicability or practicability of such claims in a given country context. In the case of Ghana, my research has focused on the nature of the actors as well as the nature of the policies that are being promoted under the new framework. The following analysis is derived from my interviews with a variety of stakeholders and review of relevant policy and archival documents. In terms of the policy making process, it is clear that compared to the structural adjustment policies, at least procedurally, the poverty reduction framework provides avenues for open debates and discussions on the country's development policies. This is particularly evident in various consultation sessions and policy dialogues attended by a cross section of civil society representatives, donor agency representatives and government officials. But beyond these procedural reforms or what Jeremy Gould calls 'populist neoliberalism'[82] my analysis of the data shows that the new poverty reduction framework does not offer any significant departure from the donor-influenced and externally-driven policy agenda introduced by the structural

78 Kanbur, 2000.

79 Tan, 2007:149.

80 IMF and World Bank, 1999.

81 Craig, 2006; Creig and Porter, 2007.

82 Gould, 2005.

adjustment regime. Instead, under the auspices a series of new aid instruments and policy arenas the IFIs and other multilateral and bilateral donors continue to exercise great influence over the country's development policy making process.

One policy arena that has emerged in the wake of the growing criticisms against SAPs and the introduction of the poverty reduction framework is the Consultative Group meetings which are held every second year. These meetings constitute the most institutionalized arena in which the Government and donors interact. Having taken part in these meetings both as a journalist with the *Business and Financial Times* and as a Program Officer and Research Assistant with the Institute of Economic Affairs between 2001 and 2003, I have experienced first-hand knowledge on how these donor-government 'encounters' work.[83] The quarterly 'Mini Consultative Group' provides a more regular arena in which donors and the Government meet to review the country's economic situation. There are also sectoral level arenas for government–donor policy discussions on, for example, health, education and decentralization, as well as monthly donor meetings where the heads of donor agencies discuss issues that advance the development agenda.

The latest innovation in such arenas is the Multi-Donor Budgetary Support (MDBS) mechanism. Introduced in March 2003, the MDBS mechanism brings together a number of so-called development partners that provide general budget support GPRS. The MDBS was set up soon after the first edition of the country's poverty reduction strategy was approved by Parliament, and in the context of the Government's decision to join the HIPC initiative.[84] Even though on paper the IFIs claim the overarching objective of the MDBS is to provide more harmonized assistance for Ghana to implement the GPRS,[85] a critical investigation and analysis would suggest that the MDBS and similar initiatives are among a new set of mechanisms and instruments aimed at governing aid recipient countries 'at a distance.'[86] As one civil society activist told me, 'this mechanism in particular, has enabled the so-called development partners to determine the country's budgetary allocations—a practice which no doubt, raises questions about the very essence of national sovereignty.'[87]

While the executive arm of the Ghanaian government enjoys unlimited access to donors and oversees all bilateral and multilateral negations relating to debt relief, in contrast Parliament as an institution is constrained in the policymaking terrain by structural, historical and situational factors. Structurally, Parliament's lawmaking and oversight functions are weak, making it mostly a deliberative body. The current constitution which was promulgated after the return to democratic

83 As the Features/Political editor, I covered the Consultative Group meeting held in Accra in 2002. I also coordinated the 'Mini Consultative Group' at the Institute of Economic Affairs in 2002–2003.

84 See Quartey and Osei, 2002; 2003.

85 Cavalcanti1, 2007.

86 Miller and Rose, 1990; 2008.

87 Interviews, August 2006.

rule in 1992 provides the legal and legislative framework for allocation of power and authority. The constitution established a hybrid between the American-styled presidential system and the British-styled parliamentary system.

The implication of this is the creation of an overly strong executive presidency and a weakened legislature. The Constitution mandates the President to appoint the majority of Ministers from Parliament and permits the appointments of MPs to boards of state institutions.[88] This provision has the effect of not only undermining the oversight responsibility of parliament over the executive but it renders the legislature increasingly redundant in the policy making equation. Parliament's lawmaking function is further weakened by a constitutional provision which prohibits MPs from introducing bills that impose taxes, charges or withdrawals from public funds.[89] This article severely reduces the scope of private member bills and has led to the belief among a majority of MPs that legislation must originate from the executive.[90] The Constitution also gives the executive branch the responsibility for drafting all supporting legislation that defines how policies will be implemented. A parliamentary committee has some oversight of this process, but the scope of its review is limited to accepting or rejecting it. These constitutional constraints are buttressed by the historical marginalization of Parliament. There is a legacy of the centralization of power within the executive since independence largely as a result of frequent military interruptions to the constitutional order and partly as a result of the belief in a strong 'Chief Executive' as the essence of the pre-historic political head. More debilitating than the selection of the majority of ministers from Parliament is the effect of this legacy which has resulted in Parliament ceding its role in policymaking through its inaction.[91] The current constitution follows its predecessors by giving the executive more power than Parliament.

The Ghanaian Constitutional provision prohibiting Parliament from introducing financial bills is the biggest obstacle, because without the ability to allocate itself resources, Parliament is dependent on the executive for what it receives. This dependency may be the reason why Parliament lacks research and administrative capabilities and Parliamentarians do not even have offices. In terms of situational constraints, Parliament is largely by-passed in the process of donor–government 'policy dialogue.'[92] This situation results from the structural limitations discussed above and from tendencies inherent in the donor aid system to marginalize

88 Constitution of Republic of Ghana, 1992:63.

89 Constitution of Republic of Ghana, 1992:83.

90 Many minority MPs told me their frustrations with this particular situation, claiming that even though they had initiated countless legislations their efforts have always met with strong resistance from members of the governing party who decide on the legislative agenda and have to power to decide whether or not such private members bills could be introduced.

91 Ayee, 2008; Whitfield, 2005.

92 Whitfield, 2005.

Parliament as an institution. The arenas for donor–government 'policy dialogue' are not accessible to Parliament as an institution. While Parliament is delegated constitutionally the power to approve loan agreements, both domestic and international, entered into by Government, Parliament's role is largely relegated to approving the legislative framework for policy reforms and not engaging in their formulation.[93] Minority members use the tactics of boycotts on voting or walkouts as public expressions of disagreement with Government policy, but these strategies do not leverage Parliament's participation in policy discussions. Parliament is increasingly providing an arena for policy discussions between MPs and the executive and between MPs and citizens. Parliament stimulates debate on bills both on the House floor and through public hearings and private memoranda. Interestingly, several bilateral donors have programs aimed at enhancing the capacity of Parliament and its engagement with segments of society in terms of making inputs into laws and policies.[94] The power dynamic is obvious, since it is donors who are trying to raise the status of Parliament in the policymaking process.

Under Ghana's current decentralized administrative system, District Assemblies and Unit Councils are, in theory, expected to have input into the policy-making process.[95] The essence of the new decentralized system established in 1988 and integrated into the 1992 constitution was to promote popular participation in the decision-making process; promote responsive governance at the local level; and enhance efficiency and effectiveness of the entire government machinery by making service delivery closer to the people.[96] My interviews revealed that contrary to the provisions and expectations under the decentralization process, the local government institutions have not been involved in gathering local input into the GPRS document but rather separate forums have been created at the community and district level to which District Assembly administrative staff and some Assembly members were invited. This, no doubt, is a serious drawback to the decentralization process which aims at promoting increased grassroots involvement in the decision-making process. An official at the SEND Foundation, a social advocacy group based in Accra with branches across the country, complained about the failure to decentralize poverty reduction process to me:

> I believe that based on our decentralization process, decision making should start from the grassroots. So whatever it is, it must start from there. It means that the area councils and unit committees are the ones who are supposed to gather

---

93 Constitution of Republic of Ghana, 1992:120.

94 During my tenure as Program Officer/Research Assistant at the Institute of Economic Affairs, I coordinated a number of such 'capacity workshops' organized for MPs and sponsored by donors. I also co-authored two research publications (*Assessing Parliament and Governance performance Review*, Institute of Economic Affairs, 2002) with Yaw Saffu.

95 Constitution of the Republic of Ghana, 1992; Local Government Act (Act 462), 1993.

96 Constitution of Republic of Ghana, 1992; see also Aryee, 2008.

> this information, bring it to the assembly level so that the assembly will also sit to discuss and all districts will send it to the regional level and all regions push it to the national level and it is then collated. But then, it starts from the top and trickles down and at the end of the day, it doesn't really get to the bottom.[97]

From the foregoing analysis, it is clear that the PRSP process has not significantly altered the policy making terrain in Ghana. Development policy making continues to be a largely centralized process negotiated by key ministers and public officials, working in concert with donors. As argued by Armah, country ownership in regard to the PRSP process is largely compromised by the economic leverage that donor partners continue to wield over aid dependent and poor countries like Ghana.[98] While the Bank and the Fund have publicly expressed support for locally generated policies, there are key mechanisms which hinder the ability of countries to design and implement policies based on their national interest and policy priorities. In the case of the PRSP framework, the Joint Staff Assessment (JSA) which is written by the Bank and the IMF has become one of the key instruments used to discipline aid recipient countries and to ensure that their policies confirm with the 'official' template provided by the BWIs. Also the tendency to link debt relief under the HIPC initiative to the PRSPs also meant that financially strapped governments are 'likely to opt for programs that they know will be accepted even if such programs conflict with priorities identified through consultative processes.'[99] My interviews with government officials, parliamentarians as well as civil society groups revealed this as one of the major frustrations and challenges for country ownership of development policies. According to one Member of Parliament, the newly elected Kufuor government had to 'fast-track' the HIPC application process as well as the completion of the GPRS showed 'gross disregard to the due process as enshrined in Ghana's laws and therefore an insult to the country's sovereignty.'[100] But as argued by Dr. Emmanuel Akwetey of Institute of Democratic Governance, 'unless Ghana is able to develop alternative means of development finance, any democratically elected government would do what it takes, even if it means kissing the devil to secure donor aid in order to meet the needs of the electorate.'[101] According to him, the dire financial conditions of the country have made it impossible for leaders to resist the offers from the IFIs. These sentiments were echoed by a Director at the Ministry of Agriculture, who told me that while many government officials have secretly expressed frustration over the role of donors in the country's development policy process, all the 'politicians seemed unequal to bite the bullet by standing up to these donors like past leaders like Nkrumah did.'[102] On their

97 Interviews, July 2006.
98 Armah, 2008.
99 Armah, 2008:83.
100 Interviews in Accra, July 2007.
101 Interviews in Accra, August 2006.
102 Interviews in Accra, August 2006.

part, donors have tightened their grip on aid-dependent countries like Ghana. New instruments like the Multi-Donor Budgetary Support under the Aid Harmonization arrangement have given extra leverage to IFIs and other multilateral and bilateral donors to oversee and interfere in the country's economic and development policy making processes.

New Driver, Same Vehicle or Change in Continuity?

Under structural adjustment, a combination of reform policies was implemented on the prompting of the BWIs with the aim of restoring the economy into good health and as a condition for aid. While these policies were successful as short-term measures, they soon became very unpopular largely as a result of the deteriorating socio-economic conditions of the citizenry. It would therefore be very interesting to see if anything has changed in terms of the set of policies implemented and whether or not these policies are publicly debated and agreed upon. On assumption of power in 2001, the Kufuor government made macroeconomic stability one of its key policy priorities. As a result, the main thrust of macro-economic policies and strategies under the country's poverty reduction blueprint have focused on fiscal, monetary and international trade management.[103]

These measures, as to be expected, have led to a significant improvement in the macroeconomic environment with most of the indicators including inflation, interest rate, exchange rate depreciation, etc. being stabilized. But even supporters of the government are cautious of these achievements especially given the history of how the early successes achieved under the SAPs quickly evaporated, plunging the economy into crisis by the end of the 1990s. As an official at an Accra-based Third World Network told me, 'there are fears that the new approach to development seems to be repeating the same mistakes of SAPs by overemphasizing macroeconomic stability over a more holistic and sustainable approach.'[104] In his view, 'overreliance on macroeconomic stability and market-oriented approaches as a mechanism for accelerated economic growth and poverty reduction is the major weakness of the current approach.' Similarly, a development consultant in Tamale whom I interviewed added that 'by implementing these policies without the corresponding structural reforms and physical infrastructural development would be counter-productive for the country's long-term development prospects.'[105]

There were also concerns that key macroeconomic policies continue to be determined behind closed-doors between few officials and donors.[106] These policies were hardly discussed during the public consultations and even where they have to be approved by parliament in fulfillment of constitutional requirements there is

103 Government of Ghana, 2001.

104 Interviews in Accra-Ghana, July 2006.

105 Interviews in Tamale-Ghana, August 2006.

106 Armah, 2008.

lack of full disclosure of information. Worse of all, under the prevailing political system where parliament was dominated by the ruling NPP members certain key decisions including the approval of the disbursement of the MCA funds, HIPC benefits and the sale of the Ghana Telecom (GT) to Vodafone of United Kingdom, the proceedings took a partisan twist and therefore lacked rigorous debate and discussion before arriving at decisions.

Regarding trade policy, there is a persistance of structural adjustment trade liberalization policies despite the widespread opposition to these policies and calls for reform especially in light of the adverse effects of these policies on the local economy. It is increasingly clear that the BWIs and other donors continue to pull the string when it comes to particular policies. For instance, according to Armah, in 2003 the government was compelled to reverse its decision to impose a tariff on imported poultry following pressure from the IMF.[107] Such a situation undoubtedly contravenes the principle of country ownership and seriously undermines national sovereignty. But given the country's inability to wean itself from these financial institutions there are few practical options available. My own observations, interactions and monitoring activities while in Ghana suggested that the current trade and liberalization policies are having serious impacts on local industries and livelihoods. The national economy continues to be regulated and controlled by external forces. According to Armah, 'like SAPs, PRSs have not been associated with significant export diversification. Indeed, export growth in Ghana has been driven by the cocoa sector.'[108] In fact, the post-colonial economy remains unchanged and continues to be dependent the export of cocoa beans and few mineral resources. And while Agriculture remains the mainstay of the economy employing about 60 percent, there has not been any significant attempt to develop this sector. Poverty remains a rural phenomenon affecting about 70 percent of the population, yet development programs and interventions continue to be based in urban centers.[109] My interviews in Tamale in the Northern Region revealed that unless there is a deliberate and strategic policy initiative specifically focused on the development of the three northern regions—Upper East, Upper West and Northern—the urban–rural divide would persist with its potentials for instability.

Some of these issues together with the broader topic of civil society participation and how these continue to be framed by the country's colonial legacies of 'divide and rule' are explored in the next chapter. It is however pertinent to make a number of observations resulting from the foregoing analysis. First, as I indicated in my theoretical framework in Chapter 2, and also in Chapter 3, the recent aid policies introduced by the World Bank and the IMF should be located within the politics of international development represented by unequal power relations between donors and their clients in the global South. An analysis provided by such an understanding would reveal recent aid policies and the broader international political economy

107 Armah, 2008.

108 Armah, 2008.

109 Armah, 2008.

as the present-day reincarnations of the imperial and Orientalist agenda of the West. Second, the new poverty reduction discourse represents a discursive shift in international development whereby countries of Africa and others regions of the South have been discursively produced as 'Heavily Indebted and Poor' and are in need of immediate aid from the ever benevolent West.

Summary and Conclusion

This chapter has traced the evolution of the new poverty reduction framework in Ghana to the country's implementation of neoliberal policy reforms since the beginning of the 1980s. I provided an overview of the country's postcolonial political economy and showed how as a result of a combination of internal and external factors, the country had no choice but to embrace the policy prescriptions of the World Bank and the IMF in the form of SAPs. These policies as I showed included: (a) a realignment of relative prices to encourage productive activities and exports through strengthening of economic incentives; (b) a progressive shift away from direct controls and intervention towards greater reliance on market forces; (c) the early restoration of monetary and fiscal discipline; (d) the rehabilitation of social and economic infrastructure; and (e) the undertaking of structural and institutional reforms to enhance the efficiency of the economy and encourage the expansion of private savings and investment.[110]

While acknowledging the initial role and effectiveness of these policy measures in restoring macroeconomic stability, I also showed their limitations in terms of their inability to address structural problems of the economy and serve as the basis for long-term development and poverty reduction. Consequently, the country embraced the new architecture of aid in the form of the HIPC initiative and the poverty reduction strategy papers. It has been shown, drawing on my interviews and the review of other documents that contrary to claims made by its proponents, the new framework has not altered the foundation of the policy making terrain erected by the structural adjustment framework. I have argued that while the IFIs and other donors claim poor countries are now in the 'driver's seat' in designing country-tailored, locally-owned, poverty reducing policies, a series of new aid instruments and policy mechanisms have ensured that the donors remain firmly in charge. I have argued that there are specific policy prescriptions and requirements which limit the ability of countries like Ghana to own their development policies. I strongly contend that the poverty reduction strategy framework does not offer any real departure from the top-down, one-size-fits-all structural adjustment policies. Ghana's experience with the implementation of the PRSP paradigm shows that despite a rhetorical shift from market fundamentalism to a more inclusive neoliberalism, the macroeconomic policy prescriptions imposed by BWIs on the country and elsewhere across Africa remain fundamentally inflexible. I have

110 IMF, 1991.

shown that beyond the rhetoric of country ownership as well as the procedural makeover, what the new poverty reduction framework does offer is to reinforce the undue influence of IFIs on developing states like Ghana, undermine their democratic processes and threaten their sovereignty. At best, this new framework could be seen as new governing technology—developmentality, which reinscribes the power and domination of the West over the global South, while employing subtle techniques and appropriating normative ideas. In other words, as argued by Malaluan and Guttal, the poverty reduction framework is nothing but a 'structural adjustment in the name of the poor.'[111] In the next chapter, I discuss aspects of this dynamics by critically examining how civil society as a concept and the ideas of participatory development have been appropriated and used not for inclusion and empowerment but mainly as a technology of governance and reproduction of inequality and power.

111 Malaluan and Guttal, 2002.

Chapter 5

Civil Society, Participatory Poverty Reduction and Neoliberal Hegemony

Introduction

In introducing the new aid agenda in the late 1990s, the World Bank and International Monetary Fund (IMF) had sought to demonstrate reflexivity and to project an image of themselves as 'listening' and 'sensitive' institutions, which were willing to address criticisms leveled against them. As noted in preceding chapters, one of the main criticisms was that structural adjustment policies had failed to include citizen groups as stakeholders in the design and implementation of development policies, although they were ostensibly one of the main beneficiaries. In response, the two institutions have promoted local participation through civil society involvement as a key ingredient of the poverty reduction framework. Drawing on *developmentality*, the chapter analyzes the concept of participation and empowerment embodied in the poverty reduction framework, arguing the new aid agenda represents a transformation of donor power and control exercised over aid recipient countries from top-down policy prescriptions to subtle, bottom-up donor-guided mechanisms. The chapter critically examines the various ways in which ideas about 'local participation' through civil society involvement in the policy making process are operationalized in the case of Ghana's poverty reduction strategy process.

It will first trace the evolution of civil society and how this concept has been employed by various actors and in relation to the recent aid policies. While participation has become part of the general vocabulary of the new aid architecture there is nevertheless a long history of participatory methods in development. The chapter will provide a brief background to this history before discussing the ways in which participation is used within the context of the poverty reduction strategy. For the analysis of the Ghanaian case, the chapter also draws on the work of Mahmood Mandani to frame the nature of power relations that have emerged in relation to local participation in the poverty reduction framework, and in regard to the conceptualization and operationalization of civil society. The deployment of this framework aims at unpacking the politics of civil society participation in the poverty reduction strategy process. The following questions are explored: Which civil society groups have participated in Ghana's poverty reduction strategy process? How have they participated or, put differently, what roles have civil society groups played in Ghana's poverty reduction process? Did the consultation process between CSOs and government officials during the development of

Ghana's poverty reduction strategy have an impact on the content of the final document? Are the voices of the poor incorporated into Ghana's poverty reduction blueprint? Other related issues to be explored in the research include how the World Bank and the IMF's conceptualize participation by civil society in their official documents and what form the actual participation process takes. This leads to the question of whether the participation by CSOs merely consists of pro forma consultation and after the fact forms of consensus building which could be seen as an attempt to co-opt CSOs, or whether there is genuine participation and involvement of civil society that leads to an open dialogue between governments and CSOs. The idea 'civil society' as employed within the context of the poverty reduction strategy framework serves to obscure political struggles between different interest groups to maintain control over the country's development policy making terrain. The chapter explores how participatory poverty reduction through civil society involvement has excluded certain social groups from participating in the decision making process. The chapter's analysis poses some challenges to the claim by some critical theorists such as neo-Gramscian scholars that social movements can become a site of empowerment through successful community mobilization (inclusion) and informed engagement with political structures.

Contested Conceptions of Civil Society

In recent years, researchers have widely debated the meaning of the concept of civil society, a subject on which much has been written.[1] Although the notion of civil society has become popular in current development discourse, there remains considerable disagreement about how to theorize this concept, particularly in an era of neoliberal globalization. This is not surprising, since the definition and the understanding of civil society depend largely on the theoretical lens through which the concept is being examined. In the next couple of paragraphs, I will provide a genealogy of the concept from the various theoretical perspectives as the basis for the subsequent analysis of the application of the concept in an era of neoliberal globalization as well as in relation to the new architecture of aid. Hegel provided the classical conceptualization of the civil society as formally organized groups and associations located in the space between the state and the household.[2] The concept regained currency after the collapse of the communist bloc in Eastern Europe in the late 1980s as new analytical and political tools were sought to explain the dynamics of new social organizations in a context in which the role and power of the state had greatly diminished. Historically however, the use of the term has its origins in two broad intellectual traditions.

1 Howell and Pearce, 2002; Hall and Trentmann, 2005; Kaldor, 2003; Chandhoke, 1995; Cohen and Arato, 1992.

2 Bratton, 1989.

The liberal conception of civil society stems from the writings of eighteenth century enlightenment theorists such as Adam Smith, Adam Ferguson and Francis Hucheson and later writings of Alexis Tocqueville. Tracing the evolution and usage of the term from its earliest origins, Mary Kaldor argues that civil society has always been associated with the formation of a particular type of political authority.[3] According to Kaldor the term was contrasted with 'state of nature' during the seventeenth and eighteen centuries. In that regard, civil society was closely interlinked with the state, characterized by the rule of law, fundamental individual rights, all of which was enforced by an equally law abiding political authority. Civil society at this point was a generic term for a secular constitutional order. The transition from absolutist monarchical system to the modern state was to mark a great turning point in the genealogy of how of civil society was understood. The modern state and its law and order apparatuses replaced the earlier system based on ties of blood and kinship, and religion. The growth of states and the establishment of a rule of law gradually eliminated private and often violent methods of settling disputes and created the conditions for these new forms of social interaction based on commonly accepted but impersonal means of communication. Civil society in this new usage was associated with a space where people showed mutual respect, politeness and trust towards each other. It was a society where people could engage each other freely in debates and discussions.

Also, with time, a distinction was drawn between the state and civil society. The idea of private property, first introduced by John Locke and later by other thinkers, particularly Adam Smith, identified the development of a market economy as the basis for civil or civilized society. This growing distinction between the state and civil society, Kaldor argues, was also attributed to the centralization of state authority and the increasing democratic space created for citizens to assert their rights and control over the state. This evolution of the concept of civil society in relation to the state and private property in the West was underscored by Habermas. According to him, initially in the late seventeen century, *societas civilis* was used as a synonym for the state. But the concepts became increasingly disconnected in the eighteenth century and became associated with elementary property rights, intermediate institutions, an emerging market economy and the space of societal interests protected from state intervention.[4]

An understanding of civil society in relation to the state was also articulated by Hegel, who emphasized both the importance of history and the primacy of the state as an embodiment of a collective will.[5] For Hegel, civil society was the realm of difference, intermediate between the family and the state, thus equating civil society with bourgeois society and including the market. Hegel's further conceptualization of civil society as a realm of contradiction and the role of the

3 Kaldor, 2003.

4 Becker, 1994.

5 Hegel (1820). *The Philosophy of Right*, (translated by S.W. Dyde and originally published in English in 1896) London: Prometheus Books, pp. 185–6.

state as a mediator was interpreted as overemphasizing the role of the state as a guarantor of civil society. Consequently, many later scholars, including Cohen and Arato have sought to improve upon Hegel's concept of civil society.[6] They identified civil society as an arena through which the individual was socialized.

Influenced by Hegel's work, Marx criticized the Enlightenment school arguing that the civic sphere was promoted primarily for the benefit of a single group, the bourgeoisie. In this sense Marx saw civil society as an historical phenomenon associated with the development of capitalism. Thus, the Marxist conceptualization postulated that the state was subordinate to civil society. The state in this sense was seen as an instrument or apparatus in the hands of the dominant class. The Marxist conceptualization also extended the definition of civil society by arguing that it transcends the territorial boarders of a particular State and nation. In recent years, the Italian Marxist, Antonio Gramsci, has re-emerged as an important thinker whose views were influential in redefining the concept.[7] Though derived from a particular moment in, and theorization of, Italian politics, Gramsci's notion of civil society is a meaningful conceptual framework with which to engage contemporary African political economy, and in particular for thinking about the emergence and articulation of the recent poverty reduction discourse. The concept of hegemony is one of Gramsci's original contributions to Marxist thought. For Gramsci, enduring social power and political stability are found in the realm of culturally patterned behavior whereby consent is attained by patterns of acquiescence. Through the participation of individuals in the 'myriad of social forums,' which constitute civil society, such as social movements, trade unions, youth groups, churches, charities and (some) political parties, elite groups are able to universalize their norms and values, thereby establishing a political and ethical harmony between dominant and subordinate groups.[8] In short, the education function of civil society ensures the hegemony of the elite and the legitimacy and stability of the status quo by persuading the masses to accept the political values and discourses of elite groups. This Gramscian reading of the role of civil society will be taken up in subsequent pages as I critically examine civil society's involvement in the poverty reduction process. For Gramsci, the key agents in the hegemonic or educative role of civil society are intellectuals, who operate as the 'permanent persuader' of either the hegemonic bloc or subaltern social groups. Accordingly, they serve to articulate and legitimize hegemonic discourses of political common sense or seek to challenge them through the re-education, organization and leadership of the disaffected masses. As such, intellectuals' ideas and the political values they espouse are the key shapers of popular political consciousness and are constitutive political practices.

The foregoing examination of Gramsci's notion on hegemony, according to neo-Gramscian scholars such as Ruckert, partly explains how and why societal actors

6 Cohen and Arato, 1992; See also Becker, 1994.

7 Gramsci, 1971.

8 Gramsci, 1971.

in Africa and elsewhere in the South came to embrace and articulate a neoliberal poverty reduction agenda of Western donors as the 'natural,' most appropriate strategy for long-term development.[9] Thus from a neo-Gramscian perspective, the introduction and articulation of the poverty reduction discourse can be explained in terms of not only the activities of agents of neoliberal hegemony such as the IFIs but also in terms of the educative, socializing effects of the hegemonic function of civil society. The access of a small number of urban and local elites to donor and state resources have enabled them to be co-opted into the hegemonic discourse of poverty reduction strategy policies. In short, Gramsci's notion of hegemonic role of civil society, Ruckert argues, enables us to understand how the post-Washington Consensus idea of 'poverty reduction' became embedded in the Third World development 'common sense.'[10]

Indeed, one of the remarkable legacies of over two decades of neoliberal reforms in Africa and elsewhere in the South has been the near fetishism of the concept of 'civil society.' Within the past few years, a variety of non-governmental organizations (NGOs), from local community-based organizations to large and well-funded international NGOs, have proliferated, largely as service-providers stepping in, in the wake of state retrenchment under structural adjustment and the shifting of costs to 'consumers.' This development has been widely welcomed, and celebrated as evidence of a healthy 'civil society' and a strengthening of 'democratization.' The mainstream approach to social change and development focuses on this sphere of civil society, conceived as an arena for activity, organization and association that is autonomous from the state and above or beyond the private sphere of the family.[11] NGOs are conceived as actors which operate within, or actually constitute, civil society, through serving the interests of local people using more direct and legitimate models of participation and representation than the 'top-down' structures and institutions of the state.[12]

'Civil society' also became an important term for understanding novel forms of social and political engagement in Africa where the postcolonial state was in retreat or on the verge of collapse after failing to deliver on the post-independence dreams of prosperity and rapid economic transformation.[13] While some of the elements of the classical conception of civil society may be present in Africa, the actual character of civil society across the continent is far more complex and variegated. Many civil society actors involving women, professionals, workers, students, religious leaders and rural inhabitants have indisputably acted in recent years to challenge state authoritarianism, expand democratic spaces and defend issues of public interest in many countries.

9 Ruckert, 2007; 2008; Cox; 1999.

10 Ruckert, 2007.

11 Diamond, 1994.

12 Edwards and Hulme 1992; Oyugi 2004; Ndegwa 1996.

13 Naomi Chazan et al., 1988.

Yet, as Stephen Ndegwa points out, not all civil society groups are uniformly progressive.[14] As my study of Ghana illustrates, civil society is seen by many as part of the problem rather than an agent of emancipation and social change. Before returning to the issue of civil society participation in the poverty reduction process, however, I wish to briefly explore some of the bourgeoning literature on what is called 'state-society' in Africa and its relevance for my own study.

While there are various perspectives on the relations between the African state and its societies, the one that is perhaps most dominant in Africa's contemporary development discourse can be termed the 'state in society approach.'[15] This approach, which has been widely used to explain political development in Africa, focuses on the role of societal actors or what has become known as 'civil society' in engendering democratic reforms.[16] For instance, Larry Diamond uses this approach to explain the weaknesses of democratic regimes in Africa.[17] He argues that the main obstacles to democratization are the wide-ranging state regulations of and control over the economy. Due to its control over the main sources of wealth, the state has been able to prevent the emergence of a strong and autonomous bourgeoisie, separate from the state. This argument has been extended to the economic arena where the state has been accused of hindering economic development. The World Bank in particular has based its call for the rolling back of the state on the assumption that an interventionist state is an obstacle to the emergence of a strong private sector and for free functioning market economy.

The state is seen as the source of the problem, and it must be reformed in order to liberate civil society from the stranglehold of regulation and inefficiency.[18] Thus from the World Bank's and the civil society advocates' perspective the solution to the problems experienced in Africa is liberal reforms. It is contended that when such reforms are institutionalized, a strong and autonomous middle class will emerge.[19] A strong middle class, in turn would form the basis of a strong civil society and the absence of such a class in Africa is seen as a setback not only to the functioning of liberal democracy but also for economic growth and development. Both the government and the market are said to be embedded in society. Thus the relationship between the government and the market is dependent on the existence of a civil society. Civil society complements both the government and the market in their contribution to attaining higher economic growth. Rules of the game are important, but they should be supported by society.[20]

Many objections have been raised against the claims made by the civil society approach.

14 Ndegwa,1996; and others, see Hearn, 2001.
15 Migdal, 1994; Abrahamsen, 2000.
16 Chazan, 1994.
17 Diamond, 1988.
18 Erikson, 2001.
19 Diamond, 1988.
20 Hermes and Salverda et al., 1999.

First, it is pointed out that the idea of civil society has a specific socio-historic origin, which gave it a particular connotation. For instance, in its seventeenth and eighteenth century origin, the term implied the emergence of a definable social class, with settled economic and political rights and capabilities and above all, class identity. This class, it is argued, was the bourgeoisie whose emergence also marked the rise of capitalism.[21]

The central point here is that the idea of civil society was associated with the rise of the bourgeoisie. Their struggle against the state was not merely to separate and protect the private sphere of life from state interference. It was above all a struggle to dominate the public sphere. Laissez faire in politics and the economy were the ideological justifications for the hegemony of the bourgeoisie. Hence, some have questioned claims in the literature on democratization in Africa, which argue that civil society has the capacity to secure freedom and democracy for all members of the political community rather than freedom and democracy for a dominant class, and repression for the rest.[22] Bangura and Gibbon, on the other hand, have argued that the civil society approach ignores the fact that 'civil society' is a product of the existing social structure; and that the authoritarian tendencies inherent in particular social structures are ultimately reproduced in the civil associations that constitute civil society.[23] This point becomes poignant particularly in Africa where the emerging social forces lack sufficient autonomy from the state and easily become instruments for enforcing the political dominion of the ruling elite or the prevailing attitudes and norms are regulated to a significant degree by traditional authority structures and corresponding ideologies. In either case, the emerging social forces are an easy target of state manipulation and control. Bayart's caricaturization of state-society relationship as 'the politics of the belly' vividly captures the essence of such socio-political ambiguities.[24]

The African state, Bayart argues, has become 'domesticated,' or appropriated by society. By this, he means, despite the existence of formal institutions that are more or less copies of state institutions found in the West, the character of African society determines the state's actual operation. Political actors regularly break the state's formal rules by following a logic emerging from society. African politics, according to Bayart, are characterized by what he calls, 'the reciprocal assimilation of elites.'[25]

Thus, the integration of potentially competing elites into a single dominant class is defined by its access to and control over state resources. This assimilation has made the state an integrative force in society. Ethnic leaders, civil servants, state and private sector elites collaborate with each other in order to profit as best as they can from their control over the state and its resources. To uphold the

21 Seligma, 1992 cited in Ninsin, 1998.

22 Ninsin, 1998.

23 Bangura and Gibbon, 1992.

24 Bayart, 1993.

25 Bayart, 1993.

patronage networks on which the process of elite assimilation is based, the state must acquire resources. One of the most important ways to acquire resources has been through dealings with the external world. Over the years, successive African politicians have become experts at attracting international aid. Resources acquired in these dealings and through such devices as trade policies, export taxes and the manipulation of exchange rates, have funded the reciprocal assimilation of elites through the use of patronage. Boundaries between the private and the public, and between state and society, are rarely recognized in African politics.

According to Ake, 'at one point the public is privatized and at another the private is "publicized," and the two or more political systems and political cultures in conflict may coexist in the same social formation.'[26]

The role of voluntary associations and NGOs in both democratization and economic development has also raised many questions recently. Both their internal organization and the means they adopt to acquire funding or solicit government support are hardly democratic and raise questions over transparency.[27] In Africa, as in most parts of the third world, it is not uncommon for NGOs to be set up by people in government or working for the state, in order to gain access to donor funds earmarked for civil society grassroots organizations.[28] Indeed there is now in the literature reference to Government-Organized NGOs (GONGOs).[29]

In his work, Mamdani explains political development in Africa by focusing on the state's relationship with rural society. In order to understand political and socio-economic development in Africa, he argues, it is necessary to analyze the specific forms of power established by the state during colonialism.[30]

The key feature of the colonial state, Mamdani argues, was what he calls its 'bifurcation.' In order to impose its control in Africa, the colonial state was forced to establish a dual system of government. In this system, the form of state power in urban areas was fundamentally different from that in rural areas. In urban areas, modern institutions and something similar to Western civil society were established, and power was legitimized in the universal language of rights. Here, the public domain of the state was separated from the private domain of society. The private domain consisted of citizens, whose rights were upheld and guaranteed by the state. In other words, the state was clearly separated from society. In rural areas, by contrast, state power was exercised through traditional leaders acting as intermediaries in a system of indirect rule. This system involved the co-operation of traditional authorities into the state, making them the key element of state power at the local level. The colonial state codified 'tradition,' and made it the basis of its rule. In this system, no civil society with autonomy from the state was created, and inhabitants of rural areas became subject to state rule without being able to

26 Ake, 1996:14.

27 Erikson, 2001.

28 For careful analysis and differentiation between NGOs see Weiss et al. 1996.

29 Gyimah-Boadi, 1997.

30 Mamdani, 1996.

participate in the institutions of government. In those circumstances, according to Mamdani, they became 'subjects' rather than 'citizens.'

Since independence, Mamdani argues, African states have de-racialized urban civil society, by abolishing laws that discriminated between urban residents on the basis of color. In rural areas, states have followed one of the following two strategies. Some have more or less retained the system of customary law and indirect rule established during colonialism, thus reproducing what Mamdani calls decentralized despotism. Others have sought to dismantle the colonial system, but the result has been to replace the decentralized despotism of colonialism with the centralized despotism of the central state. My own analysis of state-society relations in relation to Ghana's postcolonial political economy dovetails with Mamdani's analysis. Nowhere is the segregation between 'citizens' and 'subjects' as pronounced as the south–north divide which continues to shape and define both political decision-making as well as development planning in Ghana. Although this divide dates back to the colonial era policy of 'divide and rule,' successive postcolonial governments have been unable to bridge the divide and build a more equitable and integrated state.

The foregoing perspectives on state-society relations in Africa are critical in understanding economic development on the continent over the years. First, the legacies bequeathed by colonialism in terms of state building and society formation were complex. At independence, African states were faced with a dilemma: on the one hand, the economic interests of society as a whole were best served by pushing accumulation and establishment of capitalist relations of production. On the other hand, this entailed large-scale disruption of African societies, something that could undermine the maintenance of law and order, and state control over its territory.

As Ake argues, the political context of the development project has rendered it improbable.[31] In postcolonial Africa the premium on power is exceptionally high, and the institutional mechanisms for moderating political competition are lacking. As a result, political competition tends to assume the character of warfare. So absorbing is the struggle for power that everything else, including the quest for development, is marginalized. The result of this is what Samir Amin calls the 'crisis of the legitimacy of the state' in postcolonial Africa.[32] In such circumstances one cannot but agree with Ake's assertion that, 'the problem is not so much that development has failed as that it was never really on the agenda in the first place.'[33]

Secondly, patronage networks have largely defined post-independence state-society relations. The resources required to sustain such networks were appropriated partly through control over external trade and donor funds, and partly through indirect taxation by means of marketing boards or similar arrangements. Emergence of civil society and other voluntary organizations are not autonomous; hence they are unable to serve as a counterforce to the state. What is however

31 Ake, 1996.
32 Amin,1998.
33 Ake, 1996:1.

not properly articulated particularly in the United States influenced state-society Africanist literature is the failure to acknowledge the increasing role of transnational actors in the domestic political and policy processes.[34] Since the introduction of neoliberal economic reforms on the continent, many governments have seen the shrinking of their development policy space and the increasing influence of the so-called development partners.

James Ferguson's anthropological study of the World Bank's development projects in rural Lesotho provides a graphic illustration of the growing influence of 'development partners.' Using Foucauldian lenses to critically examine documents related to the planning and implementation of a variety of development projects, Ferguson concludes that the development industry is an 'anti-politics machine' that has both an institutional effect of expanding bureaucratic power as well as an ideological effect of depoliticizing poverty and the state. The state, in this conception, is not the name of an actor. It is the name of a way of tying together, multiplying and coordinating power relations, a kind of knotting or congealing of power. It is in this spirit that I have tried to describe the effects of the 'anti-politics machine' or 'bureaucratic state power' rather than simply 'state power'—in order to emphasize the adjectival over the normative.[35] Ferguson's work is extremely relevant to the study of state-society relations especially within the context of aid relationships where donors set and lead the policy agenda. I have drawn on his framework for my own analysis of the poverty reduction discourse which emphasizes local participation. The contribution of my work to the state-society literature is to expose the various aspects of unequal power relations embedded not only at the national political institutional level but also at the local and community levels, where contrary to the assumptions in the mainstream literature, social relations and ability to access the policy making space are determined by unequal power relations based on gender, class and ethnicity.

From Participatory Development to Participatory Poverty Reduction?

As a noted earlier, 'country ownership' has emerged as a key component of the new aid agenda. In many ways, this has been conceptualized in part to mean 'broad participation of civil society, other national stakeholder groups, and elected institutions.'[36] According to Cheru, this emphasis on countrywide participation in the PRSP process 'presents a paradigm shift from ineffective donor-led, conditionality-driven partnership to a system that puts the recipient country in the

34 There is however a fair treatment by radical literature associated with the Review of African Political Economy for example, see Harrison, 2001; 2004; Abrahamsen, 2000; Hearn, 2001.

35 Ferguson, 1994:273.

36 IMF and World Bank, 1999.

driving seat.'[37] To understand how the idea of participation has emerged from what was largely the margins or the periphery of the development theory and practice into the mainstream, even to the extent of becoming the 'new tyranny'[38] requires an understanding of the historical precursors of the concept within development theory and practice. Catherine Landerchi has identified 'three big shifts' in the debate on participation.[39] According to Landerchi, during the 1970s 'popular participation' was seen as an important component of rural development and basic needs strategies and therefore was featured in the programs of many international agencies. During the 1980s it became associated with discourses of grassroots self-reliance and self-help. Consequently, in the 1980s, NGOs came to fill the void left by the retreating state as a consequence of neoliberal reforms. By the end of the 1980s, participation had moved from the fringes of project and grassroots interventions into the mainstream development discourse where participation has been promoted by donors as a tool for important policy objectives such as 'empowerment' and 'good governance.'[40]

Perhaps, more than anyone else, Robert Chambers has played a key role in popularizing and promoting the concept of 'Participatory Rural Appraisal' (PRA) as the solution to the failures of 'top-down' development projects.[41] Thus, for practitioners and researchers such as Robert Chambers and Cornea, participatory methods offered avenues for challenging the top-down development policies that focused on notions of progress and modernity by re-focusing on the so-called 'beneficiaries.'[42] Their premise was that 'development programs are inherently unbalanced and participation can alter that power structure by adding a counter-weight to the positivist, reductionist, mechanistic, standardized-package of development blueprints.'[43] During the 1970s and 1980s many development agencies and NGOs adopted participatory approaches as a means through which to enable meaningful involvement of the poor and voiceless in the development process, allowing them to exert greater influence and have more control over the decisions and institutions that affect their lives. Thus, a participatory approach to development reflects a continuing belief in the power and saliency of bottom-up strategies in which participants become agents of change and decision-making.

It is against the backdrop of such successful mobilization and the popularity of participatory approaches that the World Bank and the IMF incorporated the concept of participation into their new policy framework. The publication of the World Bank's *World Development Report 2000/1: Attacking Poverty* (WDR, 2001) marked the formal 'big' entry and acceptance of participation into the mainstream

37 Cheru 2006:364.
38 Cooke and Kothari, 2001.
39 See Laderchi, 2007.
40 Cornwall, 2000.
41 Chambers, 1983; 1992; 1993.
42 Chambers, 1983; 1992; 1994; 1997; Cornea, 1991.
43 Chambers, 1997; 1982.

vocabulary, discourse and practice of development.[44] Also, as a part of the Bank's own effort at 'Attacking Poverty,' a massive and cross-country project called 'The Voices of the Poor' was undertaken in over 100 countries with the aim of hearing directly from the 'poor.'[45] This changing tone in donor-aid recipient relations was also reflected in the World Bank's *Comprehensive Development Framework (CDF)*. Introduced in 1999, the CDF argues that policy reform and institutional development should not be imported or imposed, but must be homegrown. Indeed, Joseph Stiglitz, who was the Bank's Vice-President at the time, described the CDF as involving 'a new set of relationships, not only between the Bank and the country, but within the country itself ... Central is the notion that the country (*not just the government*) must be in the driver's seat.'[46]

The use of participation and ownership in relation to the new poverty reduction discourse thus reflects what is described as a continuing belief by IFIs in a bottom-up approach in which participants become agents of change and decision-making. However, a number of scholarly works and policy reviews have highlighted the contradictions inherent in donor emphasis on civil society participation on one hand and the almost disregard of these groups in the PRSP process on the other hand. For instance, according to Hanley:

> Although participation and local ownership were key elements of the original design, in most countries this part this part of the process is the least well developed. In most cases preparation of the PRSP has been handled by a powerful ministry, usually Finance, which has often established panels or committees to deal with components of the document. Civil Society Organizations (CSOs) are usually represented on these, though effective participation has been varied. In many cases the number of CSOs involved is small, and even those often lack the experience and skills to undertake analysis and critique official proposals ... Consulting more widely also remains a problem.[47]

These claims raise a critical question of the quality of civil society input in the design and implementation of the PRSP. Against the backdrop of lack of technical expertise by most of the NGOs and other organizations involved in the poverty-related programs it would be interesting to explore how these groups and the poor in particular are part of the World Bank and IMF's 'new aid architecture.' It also raises the question of how civil society is conceptualized under the PRSP process. In its review of civil society participation in Uganda's poverty eradication plan, the OECD, while pointing to the effective role civil society groups have played at the various stages of the process, also highlights the difficulties that the country's

44 World Bank, 2001.

45 Narayan et al., 2000.

46 Stiglitz, 1999:22–3, emphasis added.

47 Hanley 2002:49.

NGOs have to surmount.[48] The report made an interesting revelation of how NGOs may have been exploited to legitimize the political system, not only internally but also perhaps more importantly, vis-à-vis donors. The review concludes that for the process to be effective, civil society groups need more involvement in macroeconomic decision-making.

While scholars like Creig and Porter contend that the emergence of the new aid agenda with emphasis on ownership and participation marks a move towards an 'inclusive neoliberalism,'[49] others like Abrahamsen and Fraser have suggested that within the new architecture of aid, concepts like 'participation' represent new forms of social control technologies being deployed by IFIs and other donors to discipline developing countries' political economy.[50] Like Abrahamsen and Fraser, my study draws on the works of critical theorists who have interpreted the concept of participation in terms of power relations.

Critical theorists such as Uma Kothari and Bill Cooke have proposed a Foucauldian approach to understanding power as 'something, which circulates.'[51] Defining power in these terms promotes an examination of participation as relational, something that changes based on context. Discourse on participation, they argue, must acknowledge the social construction of all knowledge and the way in which it reflects existing power relation.[52] Also following Foucault's thesis, Kothari argues that although individuals are regularly affected by macro-structures of inequality (such as gender, ethnicity, class), 'if participatory approaches … are to be bottom-up and uncover the daily oppression in people's lives and reveal their interests and needs, they need to go beyond these conventional stratification of power.'[53] In her analysis of what she and Bill Cooke call, 'the new tyranny,' Kothari argues that although the rhetoric of development practitioners now includes reference to 'local knowledge,' participation, and home-grown policies, the reality is that genuine and untainted local knowledge is nearly impossible to cultivate.[54] Using a Foucauldian analytical lenses, Kothari demonstrates that power is not merely centralized, it exists and is exerted everywhere through the 'creation of norms and social and cultural practices at all levels.'[55] Her argument that knowledge, even at the local level is not free from the social and political influences of those who wield power over them, very much confirms my own observation and analysis of power relations in Ghana. As will be elaborated upon later in this chapter, the idea of civil society participation especially within the context of Ghana does raise a couple of questions including (a) which civil society

48 OECD, 2003.
49 Craig and Porter, 2006.
50 Abrahamsen, 2004; Fraser, 2005.
51 Cook and Kothari, 2001:11.
52 Cook and Kothari.
53 Kothari, 2001:144.
54 Kothari, 2001.
55 Kothari, 2001.

groups are we talking about? The urbanized, highly educated, donor-funded or, does civil society include the village community groups? (b), how are these civil society groups determined and by whom?

During my interviews in Tamale in Northern Ghana, out of the 20 organizations I visited only five were involved in the civil society consultation. Upon a critical scrutiny, I found out that all the five groups are local affiliates of Accra-based organizations. Thus only those groups already connected with the process were invited. In other words, the selection process was skewed in favor of well-established and well-endowed organizations. Thus, within the civil society community in Ghana, there is unequal access to power which is based on a set of social, economic, and other factors. Therefore, any enquiry on civil society participation needs to uncover such power relationships at the national and community levels and particularly across the urban–rural divide. In her other works, Kothari problematizes participatory approaches to formulating development knowledge and policies by suggesting that certain voices are not heard or considered because they are not familiar with the current development techniques and trends.[56]

Thus, unequal access to the mechanisms and information required to have a valid opinion regarding development becomes an issue of power relations as well. Kothari asserts, 'Experts are able to confirm the legitimacy of their role and intervention by claiming to possess the latest and more advanced expertise ... this superior knowledge relies on constant reiteration and renewal of technical language, methods and orthodoxies.'[57] This amounts to the professionalization of development, in which 'overarching discourses of humanitarianism, philanthropy, and poverty alleviation' pose as justifications and authority that warrants intervention and the continued top-down approach to development. Some other critical theorists argue that the discourse on participation serves as a hollow goal, and that participation is merely a mask added to a project in an effort to obfuscate undesirable conditions such as continued centralization or as means to override existing decision-making structures.[58] In particular, James Ferguson's celebrated work alluded to earlier provides an interesting example of how participation is framed as a pawn and inserted into the policy discourse in an effort to appease the participatory paradigm, with little consideration for the new power dynamics that it creates in terms of who participates, and often more importantly, who is left out.

This and other critical analysis help not only to illuminate some of the contradictions of the participatory discourse but to also unmask the various mechanisms through which agents of neoliberalism continue to perpetuate their dominance of the development agenda of poor countries. My own observations and analysis of my data from Ghana cohere with the observation by Glyn Williams that uncritical application of participatory approaches can act to ossify social

56 Kothari, 2005.

57 Kothari, 2005.

58 Biggs and Smith 1998; Mosse 1994; Sirrat 1997.

norms and that, as argued by Uma Kothari there is the tendency of participatory approaches to mask the power structure of society.[59]

In the case of Ghana's poverty reduction process, methods adopted to operationalize participation are better understood within the larger context of existing practices that masquerade under the labels of participation and consultation, policy forums and dialogues.[60] The formulation and implementation of the PRSP process has been characterized by a series of consultations and policy dialogues with selected groups in society to elicit 'stakeholder' input on policies, programs and projects. The general trend in these consultations has been to emphasize process over substance.[61] They focus on the objective of consulting 'civil society,' rather than facilitating informed opinions and substantial discussion on the issues put forth in the consultations. In many cases, they serve more as mechanisms to validate decisions already taken and to contain demands for greater inclusion in policymaking processes.

As noted by Cooke and Kothari, the rhetoric of participation and empowerment used in development programs, promising empowerment and appropriate development have the danger of co-opting people to participate in a predetermined agenda.[62] And as I discovered in my field work, participation and consultation have been used interchangeably and without recognition of the fact that those who actually participate or in this case are 'consulted,' are determined by a set of socially determined factors, including class, gender and location. The dominant method of participation has been the public hearing approach, at which the quality of discussion and debate of policy issues are poor or non-existent for various reasons.[63] A number of workshops were held with women's groups, the media, policy activists and think tanks, the trade union congress and the Ghana Association of Private Voluntary Organizations. The draft Poverty Reduction Framework was circulated for comments from organized professional and trade associations.

However, the consultation process was flawed in many respects. In terms of civil society participation, the choice of groups was arbitrary. While civil society and the private sector organizations from the Greater Accra region were given ample opportunity to express their views on many aspects of the document, groups in other parts of the country, especially in the three northern regions, were not given the same opportunities. Each of the four thematic groups preparing the GPRS also had NGO representation although it was confirmed that government representatives dominated the process.

The key problems with regard to the quality of consultations involved the limited time allowed for discussions and the late release of critical draft papers

59 Williams, 2004; Kothari, 2001.

60 Similar conclusions were reached by Abugri, 2001; Whitfield, 2005; Armah et al., 2008.

61 Whitfield, 2005.

62 Cooke and Kothari, 2001.

63 Institute for Democratic Governance (IDEG), 2006.

to civil society organizations. The large scale meetings, such as the National Economic Forum, did not lend themselves to meaningful participation as participants had to literally plough through large amount of papers which they had not had time to digest before coming to the meeting.[64] Many NGO representatives told me they felt that they should have been given a chance to organize their own consultations with their respective constituencies before coming to the National Economic Forum. Since this did not happen, many felt that they were not in a position to take particular positions on various issues at the national consultations.

Moreover, some civil society groups also claim that macroeconomic formulation was done behind closed doors despite promises of greater transparency. In a nutshell, while the new poverty reduction discourse and its emphasis on participation may have opened up the policy space for previously excluded societal actors, as argued by Andrea Cornwall, the social production of this space ought to be acknowledged in order to understand the variety of different spaces of empowerment it has created.[65]

My own analysis of the data on Ghana's poverty reduction strategy process confirms Kothari's suggestion that participatory development programs emphasizing social inclusion draw previously marginalized individuals and groups into the development process but do so in ways that bind them more tightly to structures of power that they are not able to question. I argue that while certain NGO groups have been involved in the PRSP consultation process, their inability to impact the final documents shows that their incorporation was aimed at legitimizing the process and thereby giving credibility and semblance of country ownership to what is largely a donor-driven process.

Civil Society, and the New Aid and Development Agenda

Within the new poverty reduction framework, the IFIs have equated national ownership with civil society participation in designing and implementing country strategies. This however raises more questions, not only about the conceptualization of civil society, but also on what constitutes participation. While many have welcomed the emphasis of IFIs on countrywide participation in the PRSP process as a paradigm shift from ineffective donor-led, conditionality-driven partnership to a system that puts the recipient country in the driving seat,[66] the ambiguities in the understanding of what constitutes 'civil society' and 'participation' make their usage and application very problematic.[67]

My interviews and as well as review of other primary and secondary materials reveal that in many ways, words like 'ownership,' participation' and 'civil society'

64 Whitfield, 2005.

65 Cornwall, 2002.

66 Cheru 2006; Booth 2007.

67 McGee, 2002; Gould, 2005.

are nothing but signifiers without any substantive impact in changing the centralized and donor-driver policy terrain constructed from the era of SAPs through to the PRSPs. The following description of the policy reduction strategy formulation process in Ghana provides the context for subsequent analysis: The Responsibility for the preparation of Ghana's version of the poverty reduction strategy (called Ghana Poverty Reduction Strategy) rested with a special Task Force established within the National Development Planning Commission (NDPC).

Five core teams were established with particular responsibilities for providing inputs into the crucial policy framework phase. These included: macroeconomics; gainful employment/production; human resource development/basic services; vulnerability and exclusion; and governance. These thematic areas were identified in a preliminary situation analysis. Each team comprised representatives of appropriate Ministries, Departments and Agencies (MDAs), NGOs, civil society and donors. A consultant was appointed to serve each team. The teams were required to carry out their studies in consultation and collaboration with the appropriate MDAs. Concurrent with the commencement of the diagnostic studies, local level community consultations were conducted in a sample of 36 communities. Consultations included participatory poverty analysis. Consultation workshops were also held in 12 districts and six administrative regions. On completion of draft reports by teams, a technical workshop attended by MDAs, NGOs, civil society and donors was held to harmonize and synthesize teams' work into a framework of mutually supportive program objectives. The output of this technical workshop provided a basis for further study and elaboration of proposals by the Poverty Reduction Unit of the National Development Planning Commission (NDPC) drafting team. The NDPC prepared a Poverty Reduction Policy Framework (PRPF) and its conclusions were reviewed, discussed and validated during a two-day National Economic Dialogue (NED) that was held in mid-May 2001. A follow-up workshop was held for development partners in July 2001 and an instructional workshop for MDAs that same month. A final Ghana Poverty Reduction Strategy (GPRS) was adopted in February 2003.

The preparation of the GPRS fits what I call, 'elite consensuses' between technocrats from Ministries, Departments and Agencies (MDAs); NGOs and donors. It was the representatives of these groups who were charged with the responsibility of conducting poverty diagnosis for five thematic areas. A series of consultation workshops were then organized where each team's draft report was harmonized and synthesized into 'a coherent and internally consistent program.'[68] A recurrent response from my interviews was the claim that there was limited 'space' for civil participation and that while the need to involve societal groups in the policy making process has been generally well-received, the nature and scope of participation have raised serious questions: What does participation mean within the context of the PRSP framework? Who and how do they participate? Also, as the IFIs have equated country ownership with civil society participation,

68 Institute of Economic Affairs (IEA), 2002.

a related set of questions include, what is civil society and how can we understand civil society participation in Ghana's poverty reduction process?

In order to answer these questions and in view of the ambiguities involved in the use and misuse of the term, 'civil society,' I follow Lindsay Whitfield and suggest that donors references to 'civil society' in Ghana generally cover a narrow section of society comprising professional, urban-based non-governmental organizations (NGOs).[69] This category is distinguished from rural organizations which, as Whitfield argues, are typically labeled 'community-based organizations' (CBOs) and are differentiated from 'civil society organizations' or CSOs. Within the new model of development assistance represented by the PRSP framework, donors have privileged CSOs over CBOs in the form of funding and other resources including their involvement as 'partners' in the new poverty reduction strategy process.[70] During the past few years, especially since the return to democratic governance in 1993, many NGOs, or CSOs have proliferated on the Ghanaian political landscape. This is not to suggest that the idea of 'civil society' within the Ghanaian context is new or is a recent phenomenon.

A number of studies have shown that at various stages of Ghana's political evolution from the colonial era to the present, different societal groups have mobilized and deployed the idea of 'civil society' as a form of collective identity for one form of social action or the other.[71] For instance, during many years of military dictatorship in the 1970s and 1980s, a fusion of several distinct groups came together as a united opposition against military rule. These were largely domestic pressure groups made up of the Trades Union Congress, the Ghana Bar Association, the National Union of Ghana Students, Catholic Bishops Conference and the Christian Council of Ghana. Together, these groups demanded democratic reforms and are partly credited for the successful democratization movement which ushered in Ghana's Fourth Republic in 1993.[72] The opposition to the neoliberal reform policies in the form of structural adjustment programs came predominantly from this group of local pressure groups and a fusion of local and international NGOs.[73] The opposition to the SAPs and their eventual replacement with the PRSPs could be interpreted as the beginning of the process towards the reconfiguration of the 'civil society' landscape in Ghana. As an official of the Ghana Integrity Initiative (GII) told me during my field work, the shift from SAPs to PRSPs is 'a victory for the social justice movement' and also the beginning of the next battle towards economic emancipation.'[74]

---

69 Whitfield, 2003.

70 Gyimah-Boadi, 1994; Hutchful, 2002.

71 Chazan, 1983; 1992; Akwetey, 1998; Boafo-Arthur, 1998; Gyimah-Boadi, 1994; Whitfield, 2003.

72 Chazan, 1992; 1993; Ninsin, 1998; Abrahamsen, 2000.

73 SAPRI, 2004.

74 Interviews, July 2006.

This reconfiguration and perhaps, reconstruction and an alignment of social groups is reflected in the growing alliance between local elite (professional) pressure groups and international NGOs as well as a distinction between NGOs and CBOs. As argued by Whitfield, the advent of democratic rule in 1993 also represents a drastic change of the context in which societal groups functioned or operated in the 1970s and 1980s.[75] This new reality is therefore marked by the exit of groups like the Ghana Bar Association and the Association of Recognized Professional Bodies from the forefront of pressure group activism and the entry of advocacy groups.

Thus a new group of social, economic advocacy groups and self-styled think-tanks and research institutes have become prominent and are exerting more influence on the development policy making process.[76] There are debates on whether groups like the Ghana Bar Association and Association of Recognized Professional Bodies have just merely withdrawn or whether they have been co-opted and are therefore are now speaking the language of dominant forces represented by the neoliberal state-represented by the NPP government working in close collaboration with the IFIs.

My own personal experience within the 'civil society' community—in the media and later at the policy think-tank—has led me to conclude that to a very large extent the change of government in 2000—the first opposition victory in 30 years and importantly the bringing into office of the NPP which has espoused market-led agenda—has no doubt reconfigured Ghanaian social forces. To be sure, many members of the new government including the President and other senior ministers had for many years occupied prominent positions in the Bar Association and were the leading lights of the Association of Organized Professional Bodies. The electoral victory of the NPP could be interpreted as a victory for a group of professionals and intellectuals who had worked together. This fact is more significant against the backdrop of the huge number of journalists, academics and other professionals who were appointed into the Kufuor-led government (2003-2009) as Ministers of State, Regional Ministers, District Chief Executives, Members of the Council of State and Ambassadors.

One of the key concerns of the study which resulted in this book was to probe the implications of this reconfiguration in the 'civil society' landscape. In particular, the study aimed at identifying changes and continuities between the past era of collective action resulting from exclusion and the current era of the emphasis on 'civil society' participation as a mechanism for inclusion and to achieve country ownership of development policies. During my field research, I interviewed members of the two categories of societal actors—urban-based NGOs and self-styled CSOs; and rural or CBOs.

My interviews in Accra were mainly with the CSOs while in Northern Ghana I interviewed CBOs, even though there were also local representatives of the urban-

75 Whitfield, 2003.

76 Frank Ohemeng, 2005.

based groups. Responses to my questions by the two groups were unsurprising. While CSOs saw the consultation process as an improvement on the closed-door policy under SAPS, they nevertheless argued that the consultation process was inadequate and did not represent effective participation of citizens in the development policy making processes. The Integrated Social Development Center (ISODEC) is one of the new social-economic advocacy groups headquartered in Accra and with local offices across the country. It has been very much involved in PRSP consultation process. In a position paper on the GPRS, the Center points out:

> The problem of participation is not so much the numbers of persons reached, but the quality of the discussion and the credibility of the consultations. The quality of the discussions is determined both by the diversity and knowledge of the people around the table as well as information parity. On the latter, a lot has been wanting, a situation not caused merely by the government but also by the IFIs. On the part of government, few people outside Accra and a limited number of organizations have had access to the key documents and when they are provided, they tend to come too late for meaningful consultation. In fact, the GPRS has been described as bulky and not reader-friendly, making it difficult for civil society to study the draft and comment.[77]
>
> Members of the other category (CBOs) on their part felt that the GPRS process does not represent a shift from the centralized policy making regime of SAPs. They contend that civil society as understood and applied in relation to the GPRS reproduces unequal power relations and opportunities between the elite and urbanized groups on one hand and the rural and CBOs on the other hand. They argue that this disjuncture also reflects the dichotomies of the urban-rural development divide and its implications for the distribution of the incidence of poverty in the country.[78] In my interviews with a number of CBOs in Northern Ghana, there was a consensus that the big north-south divide in terms of allocation of development projects and resources still persists and that the three northern regions—Northern Region, Upper West and Upper East—continue to be sidelined despite promises to the contrary by politicians in Accra.

One of my first impressions on arrival in Tamale (Northern Regional capital) was that the Northern part of the country seemed like a different country to me. As a 'southerner' who was making my first journey to the 'north,' I felt as though I was travelling to a different country from the one I was just coming from. In fact the widespread disparity between northern Ghana and the rest of the country has featured prominently in many studies including the Ghana Statistical Living Standards Survey discussed in Chapter 4, and has been singled out as one of the

77 The Ghana Poverty Reduction Strategy (*GPRS*). *ISODEC*'S *Position Paper (ISODEC: Accra, 2003)* http://www.isodec.org.gh/Papers/GPRSpositionpaper.PDF.

78 Ghana Statistical Service *Ghana Living Standards Survey*, 1999.

potential sources for large-scale conflict and instability.[79] During my field trip to Tamale, I encountered a lady whose NGO was devoted to supporting single mothers through a loan scheme. When I asked her whether her organization had benefited from any public government support, she told me:

> Never! I don't think anybody in Accra cares about those of us who live here. I have been running this organization for more than two years and I have approached a number of relevant government agencies and departments for support, but without any luck. I guess if I was located in Accra or anywhere else apart from the north the story would have been different.[80]

These sentiments were echoed during my interviews and interactions with a number of residents in Tamale, this issue of neglect by successive governments kept popping up and it was clear that unless a holistic approach is taken at confronting the problem, this could as well become a threat to national stability and unity. Mr. Mohammed Ahmed was the Chief Technical Advisor of the Northern zone of committee of NGOs working to coordinate activities of NGOs in the region. According to him while on paper the GPRS could provide the framework for bridging the north–south development divide, there is lack of political commitment on part of Accra-based politicians to decentralize especially financial power to the districts and the regions. He argues:

> At the district assembly level, there is a capacity gap … top doesn't want to relinquish authority. Even though the law now says that authority should devolve, the central government does not seem willing to do … but if you don't start, when do you build the capacity? If you look at the GPRS process at the community level they don't know about it.[81]

These contradictions also reflect some of the broader conceptual and theoretical issues that have dominated debates within development studies. Drawing on *developmentality* to analyze the concept of participation and empowerment embodied in the PRSP framework proves fruitful in a number of ways. The new architecture of aid or what Gould calls 'new conditionality'[82] is an instrument aimed at governing recipients of development assistance. It inscribes them into a particular epistemic community whereupon internalization of that particular discourse will enable self-governance in accordance with stipulated guidelines.

Further, as the prevailing development paradigm implies participation, whatever is proposed or imposed is legitimized with recourse to being the choice and interest of the beneficiaries and recipients. Participation becomes a means

79 Tsikata and Seini, 2004.

80 Interviews in Tamale, August 2006.

81 Interviews in Tamale-Ghana, August 2006.

82 Gould, 2005.

to advance top-down perspectives as it makes recipients responsible for policy measures that inevitably has to be approved by donor institution. Participation, as a condition itself, is imperative if the recipients are to get a sense of ownership of the process and to get a sense of liberation and freedom. The paradox of this is how the same policies which promise liberation and freedom, could in fact be accompanied by certain measures, which enable donors to exercise indirect mechanism of surveillance and governance, akin to what Miller and Rose call, 'governing at a distance.'[83] To govern at distance, according to Miller and Rose, as noted in Chapter 2, describes how agents of neoliberalism emphasize self-control or self-regulation whereby aid recipient countries are made to believe that they are in charge of their own policies. It also allows agents of neoliberalism to shift the responsibility for the failure of policies to beneficiaries.

I have however expanded on this argument deploying the concept of *developmentality,* which frames the new poverty reduction discourse as a reproduction of Western representations of Africa and other regions of the global South through the mobilization of normative discourses such as 'development' and 'poverty reduction.' In the case of the new aid architecture, I argue that framing countries as Heavily Indebted and Poor justifies the West's attempt through the implementation of neoliberal policies phrased in the language of local ownership and participation. My research highlights how certain societal groups have internalized ideas of donors, believing that the cooperation into donor programs would eventually result in 'a change from within.' Ownership and participatory approaches seem to have become the main conditions of aid, but what governments own and participate in need to abide by donors' intentions and wishes. I argue that the post-Washington Consensus policy changes, which were supposed to alter power relations between donor and aid recipient countries, have had the effect of reproducing donor power—which now operates in a more subtle way.

Summary and Conclusion

This chapter has examined the academic understanding of the growth of participation as the new buzzword of development through a systematic literature review, dissecting the debates surrounding the orthodoxy of participation, revealing trends in its theoretical evolution, and illustrating the practical applications. Significant questions emerge about the way in which participatory decision-making is presently conceived by international development practitioners. There is still a tendency to focus on the best-practices model as the benchmark for successful participation. This modernist conceptualization is critiqued through exploring other models that allow for a broader framework from which to gauge participation. Following Cooke and Kothari, it is argued that any analysis of participation should focus on its transformative potentials in view of the fact that

83 Miller and Rose, 1990.

'participation can both conceal and reinforce oppressions and injustices in their various manifestations.'[84] The aim of this book, in part, is to contribute to the overall debate summed up by Cooke and Kothari that 'any meaningful attempt to save participatory development requires a sincere acceptance of the possibility that it should not be saved.'[85] In that regard, it is argued that for participation to be effective and meaningful there is a need to move beyond the cosmetic procedures to substantive policy reform that would emphasize local-level decision making. In the case of Ghana, the 1992 constitution provides the framework for policy making at both the national and local level. Both governmental and civil society actors as well as donor agencies need to abide by the constitutional provision and ensure that policy decisions which ultimately deal with people's very survival are made transparently and either directly by the people or indirectly through their duly elected representatives (in Parliament or District Assemblies).

84 Cooke and Kothari, 2001:13.
85 Cooke and Kothari, 2001:15.

Chapter 6
Conclusion: A New Architecture of Aid or New Technologies of Governance?

This book sought to offer an in-depth and theoretically-informed empirical interrogation of recent transformations in international development cooperation between western donors and aid receiving countries in the form of prioritization of poverty reduction, local participation in, and ownership of development policies. Global development actors such as the World Bank and the International Monetary Fund claim that the shift to the poverty reduction strategy framework and emphasis on local participation provide an avenue for addressing the social cost of earlier adjustment programs and at the same time helping to put aid receiving countries in their driver's seat of their own development agenda. Drawing on the Ghana's experience, the book argues that the shift to poverty reduction within the neoliberal development orthodoxy and the emphasis on partnerships between donors and poor countries, local participation, and country ownership and represents a discursive and substantive departure from the earlier versions of neoliberalism that emphasized market logic against social programs, top-down against country-driven policies; however, it also represents an attempt by global development actors and local governing and social elites to justify, and legitimize the neo-liberal policy paradigm. Specifically, the book shows how the new architecture of aid has important implications in three distinct but related ways: the discursive construction and production of post-colonial societies; the changing focus of Western aid and development policy interventions; and the reproduction of the politics of inclusive exclusion, otherwise known as 'divide and rule' in the form of incorporation if not co-optation of selected non-state actors.

As such the book provides detailed and original research on the new development paradigm; develops a critical theoretical approach to re-think conventional analyses of the new discourses on aid reform; and offers fresh and alternative interpretation of changes in international aid relations. In particular, this critical theoretical approach, which I call *developmentality*, offers a productive lens to show continuities and discontinuities in the global architecture of aid and to locate recent aid policies within the broader historical continuum of power inequalities in relation to international development cooperation and global governance generally. It also helps to problematize the self-disciplining effects of the new aid agenda as well as the changing nature of power relations within post-colonial societies in reaction to the simultaneous incorporation of political and social elites as well as the exclusion of popular voices and local populations in the development policy arena. This book thus constitutes an important contribution to knowledge about recent development experiences in Africa, and contributes to ongoing discussions and debates in the fields of International Relations and Development Studies regarding the discourses of local participation, poverty reduction, partnership and policy ownership associated with the current aid regime.

Drawing on the findings of each of the substantive chapters, this book came to several broad conclusions in relation to the questions posed in the introduction to the book. First, in terms of local participation in the poverty reduction process, it was found that the formulation and implementation of the new aid and development agenda in Ghana was characterized by a series of consultations and policy dialogues organized by donors and to a lesser extent by the government, with selected groups in society to elicit 'stakeholder' input on their policies, programs and projects. The general trend in these consultations was to emphasize process over substance. Thus, there was a focus on civil society consultation rather than facilitating informed opinions and substantial discussion on the issues put forth in the consultations. In many cases, those consultations served merely as mechanisms to validate decisions already taken and to contain demands for greater inclusion in policymaking processes.

The book's second broader conclusion relates to how the idea of local participation has reproduced the country's historic north–south divide and disparities in access to national development policy and projects. This divide was present within the poverty reduction process in two ways. First, rural or community based organizations and local government institutions were not fully involved in gathering national input into the Ghana's poverty reduction strategy (GPRS) document. This is a serious drawback to the country's decentralization process which aims at promoting increased grassroots involvement in the decision-making process. Second, Parliament as a representative institution of the people was not effectively involved in the PRSP process as it should have been in a democracy. This side-stepping of formal democratic institutions at both national and local levels suggests the unwillingness of the IFIs to reform the aid policymaking terrain. This terrain, which was erected during the era of structure adjustment when many aid recipient countries such as Ghana were under military dictatorships, needs a radical reform to reflect the country's new multi-party democratic environment, which calls for transparency and full disclosure. The tendency of the IFIs to privilege a few civil society organizations over the constitutionally mandated institutions also raises serious questions regarding democratic accountability.

A third broad conclusion of the book relates to the whole idea of national sovereignty and independent nationhood. The study of the implementation of the new aid and development agenda in Ghana showed that contrary to the rhetoric of country ownership, the IFIs continue to maintain a great influence over the country's development process, leaving little room for the government and other stakeholders to make any real input. This, the book suggests, raises serious concerns about national sovereignty. The book proposes that like the SAPs, the PRSPs framework confers too much power in the IFIs and thereby threatens the sovereignty of countries in Africa and other regions of the global South. The

IFIs, as we found out, have the sole authority to give the stamp of approval to an entire national development strategy, including its social and political aspects. This situation not only undermines national sovereignty of African countries but it also raises questions regarding the social contract between the government and the governed. It is in this vein that the theoretical perspective adopted by the book has enabled me to unpack the claims made in support of the new aid architecture. The book suggests that by emphasizing country ownership, the IFIs have not only deflected criticism against their neoliberal agenda, but more importantly, they have succeeded in shifting the responsibility for the failure of these policies or the inability to meet public expectations to Ghanaian policy makers.

Finally, a review of my field research suggests that the poverty reduction strategy framework does not offer any real departure from the top-down, one-size-fits-all structural adjustment policies. Ghana and indeed other postcolonial African countries need to wean themselves from the international institutions by rejecting the neoliberal policies advocated by these institutions. The existing power relations between African countries as clients and these institutions as patrons cannot foster a genuine partnership or the formulation of country-owned independent development policies. Over a quarter of a century of donor-guided policies have not delivered the desired results and the recent attempts at repackaging the same old policies in the form of the PRSPs has the potential of stifling local initiative and development of long-term country specific development policies. It is the contention of this study that the PRSP is an attempt by the IFIs to perpetuate their domination and influence in Africa and other regions of the global South. Ghana's experience with the implementation of the PRSP paradigm shows that despite a rhetorical shift from market fundamentalism to a more inclusive neoliberalism, the macroeconomic policy prescriptions imposed by BWIs on the country and elsewhere across Africa remain fundamentally inflexible. Contrary to the claim that this new development architecture puts aid recipient countries in the 'driver's seat' of the development agenda, the PRSPs reinforce the undue influence of IFIs on countries like Ghana, undermine their democratic processes and threaten their sovereignty. At best, the PRSP framework is part of governance mechanisms or technologies whereby postcolonial societies are produced and dominated by agents of neoliberal globalization. The book thus concludes that donors have continued to undermine policy ownership in Africa's postcolonies by imposing their own priorities and policies on African governments through new aid instruments while marginalizing the voice and participation of citizens in the process. It is argued that the new architecture of aid in the form of the poverty reduction discourse represents a move towards an indirect regulation of the economies of the global South by multilateral institutions and self-policing of these countries by themselves. This is manifested in how the new poverty reduction agenda, while emphasizing country ownership through the participation of governmental and societal actors continue to reserve the final say in the approval and adoption of development policies of global South countries like Ghana. This, the book suggested, represents technology of government whereby donors now govern at a distance. This entails new ways of exercising power by agents of neoliberal globalization. In the case of the new architecture of aid, these include mechanisms such as Multi-Donor Budget Supports, Consultative Group Meetings, Policy Dialogues and the Joint World Bank-IMF Annual Reviews. The book also suggests that the highlighted visibility of poverty on the global development agenda and the formulation of strategies for poverty reduction exemplify a broader discursive shift within the development discourse. This rhetorical shift, the study points out however, does not necessarily mark a radical reconstruction of global economic governance to ensure that the benefits of globalization are shared by all. The study argues that the emergence of poverty reduction as the new common sense and a role for civil society represent a new form of social control which is part of a broad set of mechanisms being employed by agents of neoliberal globalization led by the two international financial institutions to re-enforce the dominance of neoliberal economic agenda. These new policies, the study contends, could thus be interpreted as an attempt by the IFIs to secure the expansion of the neoliberal mode and the reproduction of neoliberal domination by coercing developing countries in particular into implementing a neoliberal, market-led policy agenda in return for receiving funds.

Contrary to the claim that the World Bank and the IMF are increasingly becoming sensitive to the flaws in their policies, the case study of Ghana shows that the poverty reduction framework continues to be framed by market-oriented neoliberal policies while the co-option of some elements of civil society opposition has expanded the hegemonic role of the IFIs. Analysis of my field data and review of relevant policy documents on the implementation of Ghana's poverty reduction strategy show a continuing domination of the country's development policy space by donors through the use of a set of aid mechanisms and instruments. The study concludes that contrary to the claims made in support of the new poverty reduction framework, there is ample evidence that in Ghana, as is the case across Sub-Saharan Africa,[1] development policy continues to be donor-driven, top-down, with limited opportunities for home-grown policies that address the specific needs of the poor. There is also a continuity of neoliberal policies that emphasize macro-economic stability and trade liberalization while failing to address issues relating to the inequities in the global economy, including fair trade, commodity prices and removal of rich country protectionist policies. Thus, my study offers a case study analysis of Ghana, one with conclusions that shed light on the implementation of recent aid policies in Africa's postcolonies.

In terms of the implications of this work for future research, I hope this work illustrates how all of us, as researchers, students and activists, could be enlisted and are already implicated in the reproduction of particular practices and representations. There is a need for intellectuals to critically engage dominant narratives and discourses on and about certain categories of peoples, societies and ways of life. In recent years, we have all bought into representations on Africa and other regions of the global South and as a result, we tend to believe that we are

1 See Gould, 2005; Booth, 2004.

more qualified and knowledgeable about these societies and on how to 'help' them solve their problems. In terms of the implications of my research for international relations as a discipline, I hope this discipline will begin to re-think how it treats Africa and other regions of the global South by rethinking how issues such as nation, race, gender and culture frame and shape international relationships. One of the main goals of my research was to begin a conversation among disparate disciplines in terms of how we think and talk about key concepts in our disciplines. I believe that there is room for more collaborative research, in order to arrive at comprehensive understanding of how different disciplines view and understand our commonly shared social, economic, political and cultural worlds. In terms of policy implications of my study for countries like Ghana, it is imperative that there is the need for a real participative development which privileges the needs of the citizenry over those of donor agencies. For this to happen, there should be a serious commitment on the part of Ghana's political elites towards a true decentralization and equity in terms of bridging the country's historical north–south divide and the growing rural–urban dichotomy. The failure of almost three decades of neoliberal reforms to address these problems suggests there is the need for Ghana and other African countries to rethink the prevailing paradigm with the view of developing a new strategy in which 'the people have to be the agents, the means and the end of development.'[2]

2 Ake, 1996:140.

Bibliography

Abouharb, R. and D. Cingranelli. 2007. 'A Human Rights-Based Approach to Economic Development' in R. Abouharb and D. Cingranelli (eds), *Human Rights and Structural Adjustment*, New York: Cambridge University Press.

Abrahamsen, R. 2000. *Disciplining Democracy: Development Discourse and Good Governance in Africa*. London: Zed Books.

Abrahamsen, R. 2003. 'African studies and the postcolonial challenge,' *Africa Affairs*,102(407): 189–210.

Abrahamsen, R. 2004a. 'The power of partnerships in global governance,' *Third World Quarterly*, 25(80): 1453–67.

Abrahamsen, R. 2004b. 'Review Essay: Poverty Reduction or Adjustment by Another Name?,' *Review of African Political Economy,* 99: 184–7.

Abrahamsen, R. 2004c. 'A Breeding Ground for Terrorists? Africa and Britain's 'War on Terrorism,' *Review of African Political Economy,* 32(102): 178–92.

Abugre, C. 2001. 'Still Sapping the Poor: A Critique of Poverty Reduction Strategies.' www.wdm.org/uk/cambriefs/Debt/sappoor.pdf.

Adedeji, A. 2002. 'From the Lagos Plan of Action to the New Partnership[for African Development and from the Final Act of Lagos to the Constitutive Act: Wither Africa?,' Keynote address at the African Forum for Envisioning Africa, held in Nairobi, Kenya, April 26–29, 2002.

Adesina, J. 2007. 'Development and the Challenge of Poverty' in Adesina et al. (eds), *Africa and Development: Challenges in the New Millennium*, Dakar: CODESRIA.

Adu-Kofi, L. 1998. 'The Impact of the International Monetary Fund and the World Bank Structural Adjustment Programs on Sub-Saharan African Women,' *New England Journal of International Law & Policy,* 4: 73–108.

Ahluwala, P. 2001. *Politics and Post-colonial Theory: African Inflection*. New York: Routledge.

Ahluwalia, P. 2006. 'Race,' *Theory Culture Society*, 23: 538–45.

Ake, C. 1985. 'Why is Africa Not Developing?' *West Africa*, 17 (June): 1212–14.

Ake, C. 1996. *Democracy and Development in Africa*. Washington D.C.:The Brookings Institution.

Amin, S. and C. Uroh. (eds) 1988. *Africa and the Challenge of Development*. Ibadan: Hope Publications.

Amoore, L. and P. Langley. 2005. 'Global Civil Society and Global Governmentality,' in Michael Kenny and Randall Germain (eds), *The Idea of Global Civil Society: Politics and Ethics in a Globalizing Era*. London/New York: Routledge.

Amsden, A. 1991. *Asia's Next Giant, South Korea and Late Industrialization.* Oxford: Oxford University Press.

Armah, B. and J. Amoako-Tuffour. (eds) 2008. *Poverty Reduction Strategies in Action: Perspectives and Lessons from Ghana*. Plymouth: Lexington Books.

Arrighi, G. 2002. 'The African Crisis,' *New Left Review* 15 (May–June) Accessed at: http://www.newleftreview.org/?view=2387.

Aryeetey, E. (ed.) 2000. *Economic Reforms in Ghana: The Miracle and the Mirage*. Oxford: James Curry/Woeli Publishers.

Asare B. and A. Wong. 2004. 'An Economic Development of Two Countries: Ghana and Malaysia,' *West Africa Review* 5.

Ashcroft, B., G. Griffiths and H. Tiffin. 2000. *Key Concepts in Post-Colonial Studies*. London and New York: Routledge.

Ayittey, G. 1992. *Africa Betrayed.* New York: St. Martin's Press.

Ayittey, G. 1998. *Africa in Chaos*. New York: St. Martin's Press.

Ayittey, G. 2005. *Africa unchained: the blueprint for Africa's future*. New York: Palgrave Macmillan.

Aubrey, L. 1997. *Politics of Development Co-operation: NGO's, Gender and Partnership in Kenya*. London and New York: Routledge.

Barry, A., T. Osborne and N. Rose. 1996. *Foucault and political reason: liberalism, neo-liberalism and rationalities of government*. London: UCL Press.

Bayart, J. 1993. *The State in Africa: The Politics of the Belly*. London: Orient Longman.

Becker, M. 1994. *The emergence of civil society in the eighteenth century: a privileged moment in the history of England, Scotland, and France*. Bloomington: Indiana University Press.

Benjamin, B. 2007. *Invested Interests: Capital, Culture, and the World Bank.* Minneapolis: University of Minnesota Press.

Bhabha, H. 1994. *The Location of Culture*. London: Routledge.

Bhagwati, J. 2000. *The wind of the hundred days: how Washington mismanaged globalization*. Cambridge, Mass.: MIT Press.

Bhagwati, J. 2004. *In Defense of Globalization*. New York: Oxford University Press.

Bienefeld, M. 2000. 'Structural Adjustment: Debt Collection Device or Development Policy?,' Review: Ferdinand Braudel Center, Binghampton University, Binghampton NY vol. XXIII (4): 533–87.

Bird, G. 2001. 'A Suitable Case for Treatment? Understanding the Debate about the IMF,' *Third World Quarterly,* 22(5): 823–48.

Birdsall, N., D. Rodrik and A. Subramanian. 2005 'How to Help Poor Countries,' Foreign Affairs 4(4): 145.

Boafo-Arthur, K. 1999. 'Ghana: Structural Adjustment, Democratization and the Politics of Continuity,' *African Studies Review,* 42(2): 41–72.

Booth, D. 2003. 'PRSPs—Introduction and Overview,' *Development Policy Review,* 21(2): 131–59.

Bradshaw, S. and B. Linneker. 2002. 'Civil Society Responses to Poverty Reduction Strategies in Nicaragua,' *Progress in Development Studies,* (3), 2, 147–58.

Bratton, M. 1989. 'Beyond the State: Civil Society and Associational Life in Africa,' *World Politics*, 41(3): 407–30.

Brigg, Morgan 2002. 'Post-Development, Foucault and the Colonisation Metaphor,' *Third World Quarterly*, 23: 421–36.

Brodie, J. 2005. 'Power and Politics' In J. Brodie and S. Rein (eds) *Critical Concepts: An Introduction to Politics (4th edition)*. Toronto: Pearson Education.

Brown, W. 2006. 'Africa and international relations: comments on IR theory, anarchy and statehood,' *Review of International Studies*, 32: 119–43.

Browne, R. and R. Cummings. 1983. *The Lagos Plan of Action Versus the Berg Report*. Richmond, VA: Brunswick Corporation.

Burchell, G., C. Gordon and P. Miller. (eds) 1991. *The Foucault Effect: Studies in Governmentality*. Chicago: University of Chicago Press.

Business and Financial Times. 2002 (July 29–August 4, 2002).

Business in Africa Magazine. 2001 'The NPP government and economic challenges,' June 2.

Cammack, P. 2002. 'The Mother of all Governments: The World Bank's Matrix for Global Governance' www.les.man.ac.uk/government/academic/cammack/motheroffallgovernments.pdf.

Cammack, P. 2003. 'The Governance of Global Capitalism: A New Materialist Perspective,'http://les.man.ac.uk/government/academic/cammack/Governance%20of%20Global%20Capitalism.pdf.

Campbell, B. 2000. 'New Rules of the Game: The World Bank's Role in the Construction of New Normative Frameworks for States, Markets and Social Exclusion,' *Canadian Journal of Development Studies*, 21(1): 7–30.

Césaire, A. 1968. *Return to My Native Land*. Paris: Présence Africaine.

Chambers, R. et al. 1989. *Farmer First: Farmer Innovation and Agricultural Research*. London: Intermediate Technology Publications.

Chandhoke, N. 1995. *State and Civil Society: Explorations in Political Theory*. New Delhi: Sage Publications.

Chang, H. (ed.) 2001. *Joseph Stiglitz and the World Bank: the rebel within*. London: Anthem Press.

Chazan, N. 1994. 'Engaging the state: Associational Life in Sub-Saharan Africa' in J. Migdal, A. Kohli, and V. Shue (eds) *State Power and Social Forces: Domination and Transformation in the Third World*. Cambridge and New York: Cambridge University Press.

Chazan, N. et al. 1988. *Politics and Society in Contemporary Africa*. Boulder: Lynne Rienner.

Cheru, F. 1997. 'The silent revolution and the weapons of the weak: transformation and innovation from below' in S. Gill and J. Mittleman (eds) *Innovation and Transformation in International Studies*. Cambridge: Cambridge University Press.

Cheru, F. 2006. 'Building and Supporting PRSPs in Africa: what has worked well so far? What needs changing?,' *Third World Quarterly*, 27(2): 355–76.

Chossudovsky, M. 1998. *The Globalization of Poverty: Impacts of IMF and World Bank Reform*. London and New Jersey: Zed Books.

Cohen, J. and A. Arato. 1992. *Civil society and political theory: Studies in contemporary German social thought*. Cambridge: MIT Press.
Cornia, G., R. Jolly and F. Stewart (eds) 1987. Adjustment with a human face. Oxford: Clarendon Press.
Cornwall, A. 2000. *Beneficiary, Consumer, Citizen Perspectives on Participation for Poverty Reduction*. Sussex: IDS.
Cowen, M. and R. Shenton 1995. 'The Invention of Development' in J. Crush (ed.) *Power of Development*. New York: Routledge.
Cox, R. 1981. 'Social Forces, States and World Orders: Beyond International Relations Theory,' *Millennium, Journal of International Studies*, 10(2): 126–55.
Cox, R. 1986. 'Social Forces, Sates and World Orders: Beyond International Relations Theory,' in R. Keohane (ed.), *Neorealism and its Critics*. New York: Columbia University Press.
Cox, R. 1987. *Production, Power, and World Order*. New York: Columbia University Press.
Cox, R. 1993. 'Structural Issues of Global Governance: Implications for Europe,' in S. Gill (ed.), *Gramsci, Historical Materialism and International Relations*. Cambridge: Cambridge University Press.
Cox, R. 1999. 'Civil Society at the turn of the millennium: prospects for alternative world order,' *Review of International Studies*, 25(1): 3–28.
Cox, R. and T. Sinclair. 1996. *Approaches to World Order*. Cambridge: Cambridge University Press.
Cox, R. and M. Schechter. 2002. *The Political Economy of a Plural World: Critical Reflections on Power, Morals and Civilization*. Routledge: New York.
Crush, J. (ed.) 1999. *Power of development*. New York: Routledge.
Dean, M. 1999. *Governmentality: Power and rule in modern society*. London: SAGE Publications.
Diamond, L., J. Linz and S. Lipset. 1988. *Democracy in Developing Countries*, Vol. 2. Africa and London: Adamantine Press.
Dollar, D. 2001. 'Globalization, Inequality and Poverty since 1980,' Development Research Group, Washington D.C.: World Bank.
Dollar D. and A. Kraay 2000. 'Growth Is Good for the Poor,' Development Research Group, Washington D.C.: World Bank.
Duffield, M. 2004. *Global Governance and the New Wars: The Merging of Development and Security*. London and New York: Zed Books.
Duffield, M. 2007. *Development, Security and Unending War: Governing the World's Peoples*. Cambridge: Polity Press.
Dunn, K. and T. Shaw (eds) 2001. *Africa's Challenge to International Relations Theory*. New York: Palgrave Publishers.
Dzorgbo, D. 2001. *Ghana in Search of Development: The Challenge of Governance, Economic Management and Institution Building*. Aldershot: Ashgate Publishing.
Erikson, S. 2001. 'The State We're In: Recent Contributions to the Debate on State Relations in Africa (Forum for Development Studies, No. 2)' International

Peace Academy, 2002, NEPAD: African Initiative, New Partnership? IPA Workshop Report, New York: International Peace Academy.

Escobar, A. 1995. *Encountering Development: The Making and Unmaking of the Third World*. Princeton, NJ: Princeton University Press.

Escobar, A. 1999. 'The Invention of Development.' *Current History*, 382–6.

Evans, B. et al. (eds).1985. *Bringing the State Back In*. Cambridge: Cambridge University Press.

Fanon, F. 1965. *The wretched of the earth*. New York: Grove Press.

Fanon, F. 1968. *Black skin, white masks*. New York: Grove Press.

Fendler, L. 2001. 'Educating flexible souls: The construction of subjectivity through developmentality and interaction' in: K. Hultqvist and G. Dahlberg (eds), *Governing the Child in the new millennium*. New York and London: Routledge.

Ferguson, J. 1994. *The Anti-Politics Machine: Development, Depoliticization, and Bureaucratic Power in Lesotho*. University of Minnesota Press: Minneapolis.

Ferguson, J. and A. Gupta. 2002. 'Spatializing States: Toward an Ethnography of Neoliberal Govern mentality,' *American Ethnologist*, 29(4): 981–1002.

Fine, B. 2001a. *Development policy in the twenty-first century: beyond the post-Washington consensus*. London and New York, Routledge.

Fine, B. 2001b. *Social capital versus social theory: political economy and social science at the turn of the millennium*. London and New York, Routledge.

Fine, B. 2006a. 'Joseph Stiglitz' in D. Simon (ed.) *Fifty Key Thinkers on Development*. New York: Routledge.

Fine, B. 2006b. *The new development economics: after the Washington Consensus*. London and New York: Routledge.

Foucault, M. 1979. *Discipline and Punish: The Birth of the Prison*. New York: Vintage Books.

Foucault M. 1980a. *History of Sexuality, Volume I: Introduction*. New York: Vintage Books.

Foucault, M. 1980b. 'Truth and power' in Colin Gordon (ed.) *Power/Knowledge*. New York: Pantheon.

Foucault M 1991. 'Governmentality' [1978] in G. Burchell, C. Gordon, and P. Miller (eds) *The Foucault effect—studies in governmentality*. Chicago: The University of Chicago Press.

Foucault, M. 1994. *Ethics: Subjectivity and Truth*. New York: The New Press.

Foucault, M. 1997. *Security, Territory, Population (Lectures at the College De France)*. New York: Palgrave Macmillan.

Foucault, M. et al. (eds) 1988. *Technologies of the self: a seminar with Michel Foucault*. Amherst: University of Massachusetts Press.

Fraser, A. 2005. 'Poverty Reduction Strategy Papers: Now Who Calls the Shots?,' *Review of African Political Economy*, 104(5): 317–40.

Friedman, M. 1962. *Capitalism and Freedom*. Chicago: University of Chicago Press.

Friedman, T. 2005. *The world is flat: A brief history of the twenty-first century*. New York, NY: Farrar, Straus and Giroux.

Frimpong-Ansah, J. 1991. *The Vampire State in Africa: The Political Economy of Decline in Ghan.* London: James Curry.

Garuda, G. 2000. 'The Distributional Effect of IMF Programmes: A Cross-Country Analysis,' *World Development*, 28(6): 1031–51.

Gendzier, I. 1985. *Managing Political Change: Social Scientists and the Third World.* Boulder: Westview Press.

Ghana News Agency (GNA). 2001. 'World Bank Programs Under Attack' Saturday, August 31.

Ghana Statistical Service (GSS). 1999. *The Fourth Ghana Living Standards Survey*. Accra: Ghana Statistical Service.

Gibbon, P. 1992. 'Structural Adjustment and the Pressure Toward Multipartyism in Sub-Saharan Africa' in Gibbon, et al. (eds) *Authoritarianism, Democracy and Adjustment: The Politics of Economy Reforms in Africa.* Uppsala: Scandinavian Institute of African Studies.

Gill, S. 1990. *American Hegemony and the Trilateral Commission.* New York: Cambridge University Press.

Gill, S. 1995. 'Globalization, Market Civilisation, and Disciplinary Neoliberalism,' *Millennium: Journal of International Studies,* 24(3): 399–423.

Gill, S. 2003. *Power and Resistance in the New World Order*. New York: Palgrave Macmillan.

Gilpin, R. 1987. *The Political Economy of International Relations*. Princeton: Princeton University Press.

Girven, N. 2007. 'Power Imbalances and Development Knowledge,' Southern Perspectives on Reform of the International Development Architecture, 1–44.

Godfrey, S. and T. Sheehy. 2000. 'Civil Society Participation in Poverty Reduction Strategy Paper,' Report to DFID, London, SGTS & Associates.

Gould, J (ed.) 2005. *The New Conditionality: the politics of poverty reduction strategies*. London and New York: Zed Books.

Government of Ghana. 1987. *Budget and Financial Statement*. Tema: State Publishing Corporation.

Government of Ghana. 1992. *The Constitution of the Republic of Ghana.* Tema: Ghana Publishing Corporation.

Government of Ghana. 1993. *Local Government Act (Act 462)* Tema: Ghana Publishing Corporation.

Government of Ghana. 1998. *Ghana Vision 2020: Programme of Action for the First Medium Term Plan (1997–2000)*. Accra: National Development Planning Commission.

Government of Ghana. 2001. *The budget statement and economic policy of the government of Ghana for the 2001 fiscal year*, presented by the Minister of Finance, March 9, 2001.

Government of Ghana. 2003. *Ghana Poverty Reduction Strategy Paper* (GPRS) http://siteresources.worldbank.org/GHANAEXTN/Resources/Ghana_PRSP.pdf.

Government of Ghana. 2003. *Ghana Millennium Development Goals (MDGs) Report* http://www.undp.org/mdg/ghana_report.pdf.

Graig, D. 2006 Development beyond neoliberalism?: governance, poverty reduction and political economy. New York: Routledge.

Gramsci, A. 1971. *Selections from the Prison Notebooks*. New York: International Publishers.

Green, R. 1998. 'A Cloth Untrue: The Evolution of Structural Adjustment in Sub-Saharan Africa,' *Journal of International Affairs,* 52(1): 207–34.

Greig, A. et al. 2007. *Challenging Global Inequality: Development Theory and Practice in the 21st Century*. New York: Palgrave.

Grosh, B. 1994. 'Through the Structural Adjustment Minefield: Politics in an Era of Economic Liberalization' in Widner, J. (ed.) *Economic Change and Political Liberalization in Sub-Saharan Africa*. Baltimore: John Hopkins University Press.

Gyimah-Boadi, E. 1997. 'Civil Society in Africa: the Good, the Bad, the Ugly,' *civnet.org/journal* (May 1997).

Hall, J. and F. Trentmann (eds). 2005. *Civil Society: A Reader in History, Theory and Global Politics*. New York: Palgrave Macmillan.

Hanley, E. 2002. 'Thinking and doing things about poverty II: the poverty reduction strategy process in Africa,' *Progress in Development Studies*, 2(1): 47–51.

Harrison, G. 2001. 'Post-conditionality politics and administrative reform: reflections of the cases of Uganda and Tanzania,' *Development and Change*, 32, 657–79.

Harvey, D. 2006. 'Neo-Liberalism as Creative Destruction,' Geografiska Annaler Series B: *Human Geography* 88: 145–58.

Hayek, F. 1944. *The Road to Serfdom*. Chicago: University of Chicago Press.

Hearn, J. 2001. 'The Uses and Abuses of Civil Society in Africa,' *Review of African Political Economy*, (28)87, 43–53.

Hegel, 1820. *The Philosophy of Right*, (translated by S.W. Dyde and originally published in English in 1896). London: Prometheus Books.

Herbst, J. 1993. *The Politics of Reform in Ghana, 1982–1991*. Berkeley: University of California Press.

Hermes, N. and W. Salverda. (eds) 1999. 'State, Society and Development: Lessons for Africa,' (CDS Research Report No).

Hettne, B. (ed.) 1995. *International Political Economy: Understanding Global Disorder.* London: Zed Books.

Hindess, B. 2005. 'Politics as Government: Michel Foucault's Analysis of Political Reason,' *Alternatives* 30.

Hoogvelt, A. 2001. *Globalization and the postcolonial world: the new political economy of development*. Basingstoke: Palgrave.

Hutchful, E. 2002. Ghana's Adjustment Experience: The Paradox of Reform, Geneva, United Nations Research Institute for Social Development.

Ilcan, S. and L. Phillips. 2006. 'Global Developmentalities,' Keynote Address delivered before the Technocracy @ Development Conference, The University of Wageningen, The Netherlands, 26–28 June http://www.ceres.wur.nl/old%20website/summerschool/papers/Global%20Developmentalities%20Keynote%20Address%202006.doc.

Ilcan, S. and L. Phillips. 2007. 'Developmentalities and Calculative Practices: The Millennium Development Goals,' *Antipode.* 42(4).

Illich, I. 1997. 'Development as Planned Poverty' in R. Majid and V. Bawtree (eds) *The Post-Development Reader.* London: Fernwood Publishing.

Institute for Democratic Governance (IDEG). 2006. 'The Ghana Poverty Reduction Strategy (GPRS, 2003–2005): Challenges of Implementation and Assessment,' Working Paper 1.

International Monetary Fund and International Development Association. 2002a. 'Review of the Poverty Reduction Strategy Paper (PRSP) Approach: Main Findings,' www.imf.org/external/np/prspgen/review/2002/031502a.pdf.

International Monetary Fund and International Development Association. 2002b. 'Review of the Poverty Reduction Strategy Paper Approach: Early Experience with Interim PRSPs and Full PRSPs,' www.imf.org/external/np/prspgen/review/2002/032602a.pdf.

International Monetary Fund and World Bank. 2002. 'External Comments and Contributions on the Joint Bank/Fund Staff Review of the PRSP Approach,' www.imf.org/external/np/prspgen/review/2002/comm/v2.pdf.

ISODEC. 'The Ghana Poverty Reduction Strategy (GPRS) ISODEC's position paper,' www.isodec. gh/papers/GPRS position paper. PDF.

Jonah, K. 1989. 'Changing relations between IMF and the Government of Ghana: 1960–1987' in E. Hanson and K. Ninsin (eds) *The state, development and politics in Ghana.* London: CODESRIA, 94–115.

Kaldor, M. 2003. *Global Civil Society: An Answer to War*. Cambridge: Polity Press.

Kanbur, R. 1995. 'Welfare Economics, Political Economy, and Policy Reform in Ghana,' *African Development Review*, 7(1): 35–49.

Kanbur, R. 2000. 'Aid conditionality and debt in Africa' in Tarp and Hjertholm (eds) *Foreign Aid and Development: Lessons and Directions for the Future.* London and New York: Routledge.

Keohane, R. 1984. *After Hegemony: Cooperation and Discord in the World Political Economy*. Princeton: Princeton University Press.

Keohane, R. and L. Martin. 2003. 'Institutional Theory as a Research Program,' in C. Elman and M. Elman (eds), *Progress in International Relations Theory.* Cambridge: MIT Press.

Keohane, R. and J. Nye 1998. 'Power and Interdependence in the Information Age,' *Foreign Affairs*, 77(5): 81–94.

Killick, T. and C. Abugre, 2001. 'Institutionalizing the PRSP approach in Ghana,' Strategic Partnership with Africa, September 26, 2001.

Kim, K. 2005. 'Development crisis in Sub-Saharan Africa: globalization, adjustment and the roles of international institutions' in John-ren Chen and David Sapsford (eds), *Global Development and Poverty Reduction.* Cheltenham, UK and Northampton, MA: Edward Elgar.

Klugman, J. (ed.) 2002. *A Sourcebook for Poverty Reduction Strategies.* Washington D.C.: The World Bank.

Kothari, U. 2001. 'Power, Knowledge and Social Control in Participatory Development' in B. Cooke and U. Kothari, *Participation: The New Tyranny?*. London: Zed Books.

Kothari, U. 2002. 'Feminist and Postcolonial Challenges to Development' in M. Minogue and U. Kothari (eds), *Theory and Practice: Critical Perspectives*. London: Palgrave.

Kothari, U. 2005. 'Authority and Expertise: The Professionalisation of International Development and the Ordering of Dissent,' *Antipode,* 37: 425–46.

Laderchi, C. 2007. 'Participatory Methods in the Analysis of Poverty: a Critical Review' in F. Stewart, R. Saith and Harriss-White (eds), *Defining Poverty In the Developing World.* New York: Palgrave.

Larner, W. and W. Walters. (eds) 2004. *Global Governmentality: Governing International Spaces*. London and New York, Routledge.

Lasswell, H. 1936. *Politics: Who Gets What, When, How?*. New York: McGraw-Hill.

Lemke, T. 2001. 'The birth of bio-politics: Michel Foucault's lecture at the College de France on Neo-liberal governmentality,' *Economy and Society,* 30: 190–207.

Leys, C. 1994. 'Confronting the African Tragedy,' *New Left Review*, I (204): 33–47.

Lie, J. 2005a. 'Developmentality, Poverty and Politics: cases from Uganda.' Paper presented at The Public Reconfigured. The Production of Poverty in an Age of Advancing Liberalism held at Baroniet Rosendal September 23–25, 2005 as part of the Poverty Politics research program.

Lie, J 2005b. 'Reproduction of Development's Trusteeship and Discursive Power.' Paper presented at the PhD course Globalization of Epistemologies and Epistemologies of Globalization. Course arranged by IMER, Department of Social Anthropology and Department of Sociology at the University of Bergen, September 8–10, 2005 (Accessible at www.worldbank.org/sup).

Lie, J. 2011. Developmentality. Indirect governance within the aid sector with focus on World Bank-Uganda relations. PhD thesis, University of Bergen.

McGee, R., J. Levene and A. Hughes, A. 2000. 'Assessing Participation in Poverty Reduction Strategy Papers: A Desk-Based Synthesis of Experiences in Sub-Saharan Africa.' Research Report 52, Brighton, Institute of Development Studies at the University of Sussex.

McGee, R. and A. Norton, 2000. 'Participation in Poverty Reduction Strategies: A Synthesis of Experiences with Participatory Approaches to Policy Design, Implementation and Monitoring,' Working Paper 109. Brighton: Institute of Development Studies at the University of Sussex.

Malaluan, J. and S. Guttal. 2002. 'Structural Adjustment in the Name of the Poor: The PRSP Experience in the Lao PDR, Cambodia and Vietnam.' www.focusweb.org/publications/Research and Policy papers/2002/PRSP.pdf.

Maloka, E. (ed.) 2002. *Africa's Development Thinking Since Independence: A Reader*. Pretoria, Africa: Institute of South Africa.

Mamdani, M. 1996. *Citizen and Subject: Contemporary Africa and the Legacy of Late Colonialism.* Princeton: Princeton University Press.

Martinez-Diaz, L. 2004 'Pathways Through Financial Crisis: Indonesia,' Oxford Global Economic Governance program working paper (revised June 2006).
Mawdsley, E. 2007. 'The millennium challenge account: Neo-liberalism, poverty and security,' *Review of International Political Economy*, 14(3): 487–509.
Mawuko-Yevugah, L. 2007. 'In the Driver's Seat? Donors, Civil Society Participation and Country Ownership of the Poverty Reduction Strategy in Ghana.' *The Economic and Social Rights Review* (ESR Review), 8(4): 9–14.
Mawuko-Yevugah, L 2010. 'Governing Through Developmentality: The Politics of International Aid Reform and the (Re)Production of Power, Neoliberalism and Neocolonial Interventions in Ghana.' Unpublished PhD dissertation, University of Alberta, Canada.
Mawuko-Yevugah, L. 2013. *African Time: Essays on Contemporary Politics and Governance*. Bloomington: AuthorHouse.
Mazrui, A. 2001. 'Kwame Nkrumah and the Triple Heritage in the Shadow of Globalization, First Lecture,' Aggrey-Fraser-Guggisberg Memorial lectures University of Ghana Legon, Accra, 2002 (Accessible at http://igcs.binghamton.edu/igcs_site/dirton15.htm).
Mbembe, A. 2001. *On the Postcolony*. Berkeley: University of California Press.
Migdal, Joel. 1994. 'The state in society: an approach to struggles for domination' in J. Migdal et al. (eds), *State Power and Social Forces: Domination and Transformation in the Third World*. Cambridge and New York: Cambridge University Press.
Migdal, J. et al. (eds) 1994. *State Power and Social Forces*. Cambridge: Cambridge University Press.
Mkandawire, T. 2001. 'Thinking about Developmental States in Africa,' *Cambridge Journal of Economics* (2)5.
Mkandawire, T. 2005. 'Maladjusted African Economies and Globalization,' *African Development,* 30 (1&2): 1–33.
Miller, P. and N. Rose. 2008. *Governing the Present*. Cambridge: Polity.
Mittelman, J. 2000. *The Globalization Syndrome: Transformation and Resistance*. Princeton: Princeton University Press.
Mittelman, J. 2004. 'What Is Critical Globalization Studies?,' *International Studies Perspectives,* 5(3): 219–30.
Mohan, G. et al. 2000. *Structural Adjustment: theory, practice and impacts*. London and New York: Routledge.
Mosse, D. 2005a. 'Global governance and the ethnography of international aid' in Mosse and D. Lewis (eds), *The Aid Effect: Giving and Governing in international development*. London and Ann Arbor, MI: Pluto Press.
Mudimbe, V. 1988. *The Invention of Africa*. Bloomington: Indiana University Press.
Murphy, G. 2000. 'Global Governance: Poorly Done and Poorly Understood,' *International Affairs*, 76(4): 789–803.
Nadesan, M. 2008. *Governmentality, Biopower, and Everyday Life*. New York and London: Routledge.

Narayan, D. et al. 2000. *Voices of the Poor: Crying out for Change*. Washington D.C.: The World Bank.

Ndegwa, S. 1996. *The Two Faces of Civil Society: NGOs and Politics in Africa*. West Hertford, Conn.: Kumarian Press.

New Patriotic Party (NPP). 2000. *An Agenda for Positive Change: Manifesto of the New Patriotic Party*. Accra: New Patriotic Party.

Ninsin, K. 1998. *Ghana: Transition to Democracy*. Accra: Freedom Publications.

Nkrumah, K. 1957. *Ghana: the autobiography of Kwame Nkrumah*. New York: Nelson.

Nkrumah, K. 1963. *Africa Must Unite*. London: Heinemann.

Nkrumah, K. 1965. *Neo-colonialism: The Last Stage of Imperialism*. London: Panaf Books Ltd.

Nyamugasira, W. and R. Rowden. 2002. 'New Strategies, Old Loans: Do the New IMF and World Bank Loans Support Countries's Poverty Reduction Strategies,' http://www.brettonwoodsproject.org/topic/adjustment/uganda%20 PRSP-PRSCPRGF%20Analysis.pdf.

OECD. 2003. *Ownership and Partnership: What Role for Civil Society in the Poverty Reduction Strategies?*. Paris: OECD Publications.

Ohemeng, F. 2005. 'Getting the state right: think-tanks and dissemination of New Public Management ideas in Ghana,' *The Journal of Modern African Studies,* 43: 443–65.

Olssen, M. 2003. 'Structuralism, Post-structuralism, Neo-liberalism: Assessing Foucault's Legacy,' *Education Policy,* 18(2): 189–202.

Oquaye, M. 1980. *Politics in Ghana: 1972–1979*. Accra: Tornado Publications.

Osei, R., and P. Quartey, 2001. 'The HIPC Initiative and Poverty Reduction in Ghana: An Assessment,' Paper prepared for the WIDER Conference on Debt Relief, Helsinki, August 17–18.

Owusu, F. 2003. 'Pragmatism and the Global Shift from Dependency to Neoliberalism: The World Bank and Development Policy in Africa,' *World Development* 31(10): 1655–72.

Owusu, F. 2006. 'Discourses on Development: From Dependency to Neoliberalism' in M. Smith (ed.) *Beyond the 'African Tragedy': Discourses on Development and the Global Economy*. Burlington/Aldershot: Ashgate Publishing.

Oxfam. 2001. 'Are PRSPs working? Oxfam's Contribution to the World Bank/ IMF PRSP Review Process,' www.oxfam.org.

Oxfam. 2004. *From 'Donorship' to 'Ownership'? Moving Towards PRSPs Round Two*. www.oxfam.org.

Oyewùmí, O. 1997. *The invention of women: making an African sense of Western gender discourses*. Minneapolis: University of Minnesota Press.

Parajuli, P. 1991. 'Power and Knowledge in Development Discourse: New Social Movements and the State in India,' *International Social Science Journal,* 43: 173–89.

Parpart, J. 2002. 'Lessons from the Field: Rethinking Empowerment, Gender and Development from a Post-(Post-?) Development Perspective' in K. Saunders

(ed.) *Feminist Post-Development Thought: Rethinking Modernity, Post-Colonialism & Representation*. London: Zed Books.
Pastor, M. and C. Wise, 1999 'The Politics of Second-Generation Reform,' Journal of Democracy 10(3): 34–48.
Peet, R. 2007. *Geography of Power: the Making of Global Economic Policy*. New York and London: Zed Books.
Pender, J. 2001. 'From Structural Adjustment to Comprehensive Development Framework: Conditionality Transformed?,' *Third World Quarterly*, 22(3): 397–411.
Pender, J. 2007. 'Country Ownership: The Evasion of Donor Responsibility' in J. Bickerton et al. (eds), *Politics without Sovereignty*. UCL: UCL Press.
Quist-Adade, C. 2007. 'Kwame Nkrumah, the Big Six, and the Fight for Ghana's independence,' *The Journal of Pan-African Studies*, 1 (9): 224–36 http://www.jpanafrican.com/docs/vol1no9/Ghana50thCanada.pdf.
Rodrik, D. 1999. 'The New Global Economy and Developing Countries: Making Openness' Work, *Policy Essay* no.24, Washington D.C., ODC.
Rose, N. 1999. *Powers of Freedom: Reframing Political Though*. Cambridge: Cambridge University Press.
Rose, N. 2000. 'Governing liberty' In R. Ericson and N. Stehr (eds), *Governing modern societies*, Toronton: Toronto University Press.
Rose, N., P. O'Malley and M. Valverde. 2006. 'Governmentality,' *Annual Review of Law and Social Science*, 2: 83–104.
Rostow, W. 1960. *The Stages of Economic Growth: A Non-Communist Manifesto*. Cambridge: Cambridge University Press.
Rothchild, D. 1991. *Ghana: The Political Economy of Recovery*. Boulder, Col.: Lynne Rienner.
Ruckert, A. 2007. 'Producing Neoliberal Hegemony? A Neo-Gramscian Analysis of the Poverty Reduction Paper (PRSP) in Nicaragua,' *Studies in Political Economy*, 79, Spring 2007.
Ruckert, A. 2008. 'Transnational Governance Through Inclusive Neoliberalism: The International Financial Institutions and the Poverty Reduction Strategy Papers (PRSPs) in Nicaragua and Honduras,' PhD Dissertation, Carleton University, June 2008.
Rupert, M. 1995. *Producing Hegemony: The Politics of Mass Production and American Global Power*. Cambridge: Cambridge University Press.
Sachs, J. 2005. *The End of Poverty: Economic Possibilities for our time*: New York: The Penguin Group.
Sachs, W. (ed.) 1992. *The Development Dictionary: A Guide to Knowledge as Power*. London: Zed Books.
Said, E. 1978. *Orientalism*. New York: Vintage Books.
SAPRIN, 2004. *Structural Adjustment: The Policy Roots of Economic Crisis, Poverty and Inequality*. London and New York: Zed Books.
Scholte, J. (ed.) 2002. *Civil Society and Global Finance*. New York: Routledge.

Schraeder, P. 2004. *African politics and society: a mosaic in transformation*. Belmont, CA: Thomson/Wadsworth.

Scott, D. 1995. 'Colonial governmentality,' *Social Text*, 43: 191–220.

Semyonov, A. 2003. 'The Millennium Challenge Account: A New Way to Conceive of Foreign Aid?,' *The National Interest,* June 25, 2003 (Accessed at: http://inthenationalinterest.com/Articles/Vol2Issue25/Vol2Issue25Semyonov.html).

Sen, A. 1999. *Development as Freedom*. Oxford: Oxford University Press.

Seshamani, V. 2002. 'Zambia: Poverty Reduction Strategy Paper 2002–2004,' www.prsp-watch.de/publikationen/archiv/sesh_zam__prsp.pdf.

Shanin, T. 1997. 'The Idea of Progress' in M. Rahnema et al. (eds), *The Post-Development Reader*. London: Fernwood Publishing.

Shillington, K. 1992. *Ghana and the Rawlings Factor*. London: Macmillan Press.

Smith, M. (ed.) 2003. *Globalizing Africa*. Trenton, NJ: Africa World Press.

Smith, M. (ed.) 2006. *Beyond the 'African Tragedy': Discourses on Development and the Global Economy*. Burlington/Aldershot: Ashgate Publishing.

Smith, M. 2008. 'Rethinking Poverty in a Global Era' in J. Brodie and S. Rein (eds), *Critical Concepts: an introduction to politics* (4th edition). Toronto: Pearson Education.

Soederberg, S. 2004. *The Politics of the New International Financial Architecture: Reimposing Neoliberal Domination in the Global South*. London and New York: Zed Books.

Soederberg, S. 2004. 'American Empire and "Excluded States": The Millennium Challenge Account and the Shift to Pre-Emptive Development,' *Third World Quarterly,* 25: 279–302.

Soederberg, S. 2006. *Global Governance in Question: Empire, Class and the New Common Sense in Managing North-South Relations*. Winnipeg: Arbeiter Ring Publishing.

South Centre 2004. *Operationalizing the Concept of Policy Space in the UNCTAD XI Mid-Term Review Context*. Geneva: South Centre.

Spivak, G. 1998. 'Can the Subaltern Speak?' in C. Nelson and L. Grossberg (eds), *Marxism and the Interpretation of Culture*. Urbana: University of Illinois Press.

Stein, H. 2003. 'Rethinking African Development' in H. Chang (ed.), Rethinking Development Economics. London: Anthem Press.

Stewart, F. and M. Wang, 2006. 'Do PRSPs empower poor countries and disempower the World Bank, or is it the other way round?' in G. Ranis et al., *Globalization and the Nation State: The impact of the IMF and the World Bank*. London and New York: Routledge.

Stiglitz, J. 1998. 'More Instruments and Broader Goals: Moving Toward the Post-Washington Consensus,' WIDER Annual Lectures. http://www.wider.unu.edu/publications/annual-lectures/annual-lecture-1998.pdf.

Stiglitz, J. 2000. 'Introduction' in C. Gilbert and D. Vines (eds), *The World Bank: Structure and Policies*. Cambridge: Cambridge University Press.

Stiglitz, J. 2002. *Globalization and its Discontents*. New York: W.W. Norton & Co.

Stiglitz, J. 2003. *The Roaring Nineties: a new history of the world's most prosperous decade*. New York: W.W. Norton.

Sylvester, C. 1999. 'Development studies and postcolonial studies: disparate tales of the Third World,' *Third World Quarterly* 20(4): 703–21.

Tan, C. 2007. 'The poverty of amnesia: PRSPs in the legacy of structural adjustment' in Stone and Wright (eds), *The World Bank and Governance: A Decade of Reform and Reaction*. New York: Routledge.

Tan, C. 2011. 'The New Biopower: Poverty Reduction Strategy Papers and the obfuscation of international collective responsibility,' *Third World Quarterly*, Vol. 32, No. 6, 1039–56.

Taylor, I. 2004. 'Hegemony, neoliberal 'good governance' and the International Monetary Fund' in M. Boas and D. McNeill (eds), *Global Institutions and Development: Framing the World?*. London and New York: Routledge.

Taylor, I. 2006. 'When "Good Economics" Does Not Make Good Sense' in M. Smith (ed.), *Beyond the 'African Tragedy': Discourses on Development and the Global Economy*. Burlington/Aldershot: Ashgate Publishing.

Taylor, M. 2004. 'Responding to Neoliberalism in Crisis: Discipline and Empowerment in the World Bank's New Development Agenda,' *Research in Political Economy*, Vol. 21.

Thomas, C. 2004. 'The international financial institutions' relations with Africa: insights from issues of representation and voice' in I. Taylor et al., *Africa in International Politics: External Involvement on the Continent*. New York: Routledge.

Thomas, C. and P. Wilkin. 2004. 'Still Waiting after all these Years: The Third World on the Periphery of International Relations,' *The British Journal of Politics and International Relations*, 6: 241–58.

Toye, J. 1987. Dilemmas of Development: Reflections on the Counter Revolution in Development Theory and Policy. Oxford: Blackwell.

Tsikata, D. 1995. 'Effects of Structural Adjustment on Women and the Poor,' *Third World Resurgence*, No. 61/62, http://www.twnside.org/souths/twn/women.htm.

Tsikata, D. and W. Seini 2004. 'Identities, Inequalities and Conflicts in Northern Ghana,' Centre for Research on Inequality, Human Security and Inequality (CRISE) Working Paper 5, (Queen Elizabeth House: University of Oxford, November 2004). Available at http://www.crise.ox.ac.uk/pubs/workingpaper5.pdf.

Tsikata, K. 2007. 'Challenges of economic growth in a liberal economy' in K. Boafo-Arthur (ed.), *Ghana: One Decade of the Liberal State*. Dakar: CODESRIA Books.

Tsikata, T. 2006. 'Challenges of Economic Reform and Democratization: Some Lessons from Ghana' in M. Ndulo (ed.), *Democratic Reform in Africa: Its Impact on Governance and Poverty Alleviation*, Oxford: James Currey Ltd.

Tsikata Y. 2001. 'Aid and Reform in Ghana' in S. Devarajan, D. Dollar and T. Holmgren (eds), *Aid & Reform in Africa.* World Bank: Washington D.C.

UNCTAD. 2004. *São Paulo Consensus*, TD/410, June 25.

United Nations Conference on Trade and Development (UNCTAD), 2002. *Economic Development in Africa. From Adjustment to Poverty Reduction: What is New.* http://www.unctad.org/en/docs/pogdsafricad2.en.pdf.

United Nations Development Program (UNDP). 2001. *UNDP Review of the Poverty Reduction Strategy Paper (PRSP)*. New York: UNDP.

Venn, C. 2006. *The postcolonial challenge: towards alternative worlds*. London: Thousand Oaks/California: SAGE Publications.

Wade, R. 2005. 'What Strategies Are Viable for Developing Countries Today? The World Trade Organization and the Shrinking of 'Development Space' in K. Gallagher, *Putting Development First: the Importance of Policy Space in the WTO and International Financial Institutions*. London: Zed Books.

Weber, H. 2004. 'Reconstituting the "Third World"? Poverty Reduction and Territoriality in the Global Politics of Development,' *Third World Quarterly,* 25(1): 187–206.

Weisbrot, M. 2001. 'Growth May Be Good for the Poor—But are IMF and World Bank policies Good for Growth?,' Briefing Paper, Centre for Economic and Policy Research (CEPR). http://www.cepr.net/globalization/Growth_May_Be_Good_for_the_Poor.htm.

Weiss, T. and L. Gordenker. (eds) 1996. *NGOs, the UN, and Global Governance.* Boulder, CO.: Lynne Rienner Publishing.

Widner, J. (ed.) 1994. *Economic change and political liberalization in Sub-Saharan Africa*. Baltimore: John Hopkins University Press.

Whitfield, L. 2005. 'Trustees of Development from Conditionality to Governance: Poverty Reduction Strategy Papers in Ghana,' *Journal of Modern African Studies,* 43(4): 641–64.

Whitfield, L. 2006. 'The Politics of Urban Water Reform in Ghana,' *Review of African Political Economy,* 33(109): 425–48.

Wilks, A. and F. Lefrancois. 2002. *Blinding with Science or Encouraging Debate?: How World Bank Analysis Determines PRSP Policies*. www.brettonwoodsproject.org/topic/adjustment/blinding/blindful.pdf.

Willhelmson, J. 2000. *The Washington Consensus.* Washington D.C.: The World Bank.

Williamson, J. 1990. 'What Washington Means by Policy Reform' in John Williamson (ed.), *Latin American Adjustment: How Much Has Happened?.* Washington, D.C.: Institute for International Economics.

Wise, C. and M. Pastor. 2000. 'The Politics of Second Generation Reform,' *Journal of Democracy* 10(3): 34–48.

Wolf, M. 2004. *Why Globalization Works*. New Haven: Yale University Press.

World Bank. 1993. *Ghana: 2000 and Beyond.* Washington, D.C: World Bank.

World Bank. 2001. *Poverty Reduction Strategy Papers*, http://www.worldbank.org/prsp/.

World Bank. 2002. *Ghana and World Bank 2002: A partnership for progress*. Accra: The World Bank.

World Bank. 2002. *Overview of Poverty Reduction Strategies*, www.worldbank.org/poverty/strategies/overview.htm.

World Bank. 2004. *The Poverty Reduction Strategy Initiative. An Independent Evaluation of the World Bank's Support Through 2003*, http://inweb18.worldbank.org/oed.org.

World Bank and Ghana Centre for Democratic Governance. 2000. *The Ghana governance and corruption survey: Evidence from households, enterprises and public officials*. Accra: CDD.

World Bank and IMF. 1999. *Building Poverty Reduction Strategies in Developing Countries*, www.poverty.worldbank.org/files/building_english.pdf.

World Bank and IMF. 2002a. *A New Approach to Country-Owned Poverty Reduction Strategies*, http://www.worldbank.org/servnet/WDSContentServer/WDSP/IB/2000/05/31.pdf.

World Bank and IMF. 2002b. *Guidance for Joint Staff Assessment of a Poverty Reduction Strategy Paper*, http://www.poverty.worldbank.org/files/IPRSP%Guidance%20Note%20Sept%207.pdf.

World Vision. 2002. *Masters of their own Development? PRSPs and the Prospects for the Poor*. Monrovia: World Vision International.

Young, R. 2001. *Postcolonialism: an historical introduction*. Malden, Mass.: Blackwell Publishers.

Zindzingre, A. 2004. 'The evolution of the concept of poverty in multinational institutions' in B. Morton et al., *Global Institutions and Development: Framing the World?*. London: Routledge.

Index

For Product Safety Concerns and Information please contact our EU
representative GPSR@taylorandfrancis.com
Taylor & Francis Verlag GmbH, Kaufingerstraße 24, 80331 München, Germany

www.ingramcontent.com/pod-product-compliance
Ingram Content Group UK Ltd.
Pitfield, Milton Keynes, MK11 3LW, UK
UKHW011019180926
475701UK00004B/821